MW00872501

THE SALT FAT ACID HEAT COOKBOOK FOR BEGINNERS

The Essential Guide to Cooking with Confidence: Learn to Cook Like a Pro with Salt, Fat, Acid, and Heat

Trish Vacirca

DISCLAIMER

Table of Contents

Introduction

In the heart of every kitchen lies a secret that transforms ordinary dishes into extraordinary feasts. It's a secret so simple, yet so profound, that even the most seasoned chefs swear by its magic. Welcome to the world of **The Salt, Fat, Acid, Heat Cookbook for Beginners**

Imagine this: the aroma of a sizzling pan, the sound of sputtering butter, and the anticipation of your first bite. It was a cold winter's evening, and the kitchen was a bustling haven of warmth and love. My grandmother stood by the stove, a culinary maestro in her own right, orchestrating a symphony of flavors that seemed to dance in perfect harmony.

"Flavorful journey: Salt, fat, acid, heat unite, turning ordinary ingredients into extraordinary delights."

With a sprinkle of salt, the ordinary became extraordinary. A dash of fat, and the flavors soared to new heights. The tang of acid, and the dish sparkled with brightness. The gentle caress of heat, and everything melded into perfection.

In that moment, I knew that these four elements held the keys to unlocking the secrets of incredible cooking.

But as I delved deeper into the culinary world, I discovered that these four elements were not just mere ingredients; they were alchemists of taste, artists of texture, and architects of satisfaction. And yet, many aspiring cooks struggle to wield their power effectively, unsure of when and how to apply them to elevate their creations.

This cookbook is not just another collection of recipes; it is your guide to understanding and harnessing the true essence of cooking. Whether you're a novice stepping into the kitchen for the first time or a seasoned cook seeking to refine your skills, the wisdom of **"Salt, Fat, Acid, Heat"** will revolutionize your culinary journey.

Embark with me on a journey of discovery and delight as we demystify the enigmatic world of seasoning, sautéing, and savoring. We'll dive into the art of balancing flavors, taming bitterness, and achieving mouthwatering tenderness.

We'll explore the symphony of taste that unfolds when salt, fat, acid, and heat converge in perfect unison.

Through the pages of this cookbook, you will learn not just the "how" but also the "why." Unleash your inner chef as you grasp the profound impact of each element on your culinary canvas. This is not just about cooking; it's about crafting moments that linger in your memory, leaving a lasting impression on every palate that encounters your creations.

So, let's embark on this culinary adventure together, where each recipe is a stepping stone, and each dish a masterpiece in the making. From the simplest of salads to the most intricate roasts, let the four elements be your guiding stars in the constellation of taste.

Prepare to unlock the secrets of exceptional cooking, where every meal becomes a symphony of flavors and every dish a masterpiece. Let the journey begin.

Understanding the Four Elements: Salt, Fat, Acid, and Heat

Salt, fat, acid, and heat form the fundamental pillars of successful cooking. These vital components serve as the cornerstone, infusing dishes with irresistible flavors that make every bite a delectable experience.

Salt enhances flavor and helps to bring out the natural flavors of food. It also helps to preserve food and prevent it from spoiling.

Fat adds richness and texture to food. It also helps to carry flavor and make food more satisfying.

Acid brightens and balances flavors. It also helps to break down tough proteins and make food more tender.

Heat cooks food and brings out its natural flavors. It also helps to kill harmful bacteria and make food safe to eat.

These four elements work together to create delicious, balanced, and satisfying dishes. By understanding how to use these elements, you can become a better cook and create food that your family and friends will love.

Here are some examples of how to use the four elements in cooking:

Salt: Salting a steak before cooking helps to draw out moisture and create a more tender and flavorful crust. Salting a soup or stew at the end of cooking helps to brighten the flavors and bring them together.

Fat: Adding fat to a dish can help to make it more flavorful and satisfying. For example, adding olive oil to a salad dressing helps to enhance the flavors of the vegetables and make the dressing more creamy. Adding butter to a pan before cooking eggs helps to create a richer and more flavorful dish.

Acid: Adding acid to a dish can help to brighten the flavors and balance out the richness of fat. For example, adding lemon juice to a vinaigrette helps to brighten the flavors of the vinegar and oil. Adding vinegar to a tomato sauce helps to balance out the sweetness of the tomatoes and create a more complex flavor profile.

Heat: Heat is essential for cooking food. It helps to break down tough proteins and make food more tender. It also helps to release the flavors of food and create a more flavorful dish. For example, cooking a steak over high heat helps to create a browned crust that seals in the juices and creates a more flavorful steak. Cooking vegetables over medium heat helps to preserve their nutrients and create a more tender and flavorful dish.

By understanding the four elements of good cooking, you can become a better cook and create delicious, balanced, and satisfying dishes.

How the Elements Interact and Enhance Each Other

Picture a culinary dance where Salt, Fat, Acid, and Heat move in harmony, each complementing the other's moves. When these elements come together, magic happens in your cooking.

1. Salt and Fat: A Perfect Duo

Salt and fat are best friends in the kitchen. Salt enhances the flavors that fat carries, making them more pronounced and satisfying. Think of a buttery, salted caramel sauce or a perfectly seasoned steak cooked in a drizzle of olive oil. Their partnership creates a symphony of taste that lingers on your taste buds.

2. Acid and Heat: A Dynamic Duo

Acid and heat make an exciting pair. Heat intensifies the tangy, bright flavors of acid, bringing a lively zing to your dishes. A squeeze of lemon juice over a hot bowl of soup or a splash of vinegar in a sizzling stir-fry elevates the taste and keeps your palate intrigued.

3. Salt and Acid: A Balancing Act

Salt and acid are like yin and yang, balancing each other in perfect harmony. Salt tames the sharpness of acid, making it more pleasant and less overpowering. A pinch of salt in a tangy vinaigrette or a citrusy marinade creates a symphony of flavors that dance together.

4. Heat and Fat: The Transformative Duo

Heat and fat are culinary transformers. Heat renders fat, making it melt and infuse ingredients with flavor. The crackling of fat as it fries or the sizzle of a juicy steak on a hot grill showcases their dynamic partnership, turning ordinary ingredients into extraordinary delights.

5. Salt, Fat, Acid, and Heat: The Culinary Quartet

When all four elements come together, they create culinary magic. Salt enhances flavors, fat carries them, acid brightens them, and heat transforms them. Whether you're sautéing, roasting, or simmering, understanding how to use this quartet effectively elevates your cooking to new heights.

So, let's embrace the dance of these elements in our kitchen, where they interact and enhance each other, crafting dishes that leave a lasting impression on every plate.

With this culinary knowledge, you hold the power to create unforgettable feasts and turn your meals into culinary masterpieces. Happy cooking!

How to Use this Cookbook

Using the "Salt, Fat, Acid, Heat Cookbook for Beginners" is an exciting and enriching experience that will empower you to become a skilled and confident cook. Here's a simple guide on how to make the most of this cookbook:

1. Read the Introduction: Start by reading the introduction to understand the philosophy behind the cookbook and the importance of the four elements:

Salt, Fat, Acid, and Heat. This will set the stage for your culinary journey.

2. Familiarize yourself with the Four Elements: Before diving into the recipes, take some time to read the section that explains each element—Salt, Fat, Acid, and Heat. Understanding their roles and interactions will give you a solid foundation for applying them effectively in your cooking.

3. Explore the Recipes: Browse through the recipes and choose the ones that appeal to you. The cookbook likely includes a variety of dishes, from simple salads to more complex roasts, designed to help you practice and master the four elements.

4. Follow the Instructions: Each recipe will provide clear and concise instructions on how to use the four elements to achieve delicious results. Pay attention to the details and follow the steps carefully to ensure the best outcome.

5. Experiment and Customize: Don't be afraid to get creative with the recipes! As you become more comfortable with the four elements, feel free to experiment and customize the dishes to suit your taste preferences.

6. Learn from Mistakes: Cooking is an art, and mistakes are a part of the learning process. If a dish doesn't turn out as expected, don't be discouraged. Reflect on what went wrong, adjust your approach, and try again. Learning from mistakes is an essential part of becoming a skilled cook.

7. Take Notes: Keep a journal or notebook where you jot down your cooking experiences, insights, and modifications to the recipes. This will help you track your progress and remember what works best for future reference.

8. Seek Inspiration: Don't limit yourself to the recipes in the cookbook alone. Look for inspiration from other sources, such as cooking shows, food blogs, and magazines. Incorporate the four elements into various dishes to expand your culinary repertoire.

9. Share and Enjoy: Cooking is a joy meant to be shared with loved ones. Invite friends and family to taste your creations and revel in the joy of bringing people together through delicious food.

10. Practice, Practice, Practice: Like any skill, cooking improves with practice. Keep using the cookbook regularly, trying new recipes and techniques, and honing your skills with each cooking session.

Remember, the "Salt, Fat, Acid, Heat Cookbook for Beginners" is more than just a compilation of recipes—it's a gateway to a deeper understanding of cooking. Embrace the journey, savor every flavor, and let the magic of the four elements transform your culinary endeavors into extraordinary experiences. Happy cooking!

Note

_____

_____

_____

_____

_____

_____

_____

_____

_____

_____

_____

_____

_____

Part I

Chapter 1

The Magic of Salt

The Role of Salt in Cooking

Salt is like the conductor of flavor in cooking, adding depth and enhancing the taste of your dishes. It's not just about making things salty; salt plays a crucial role in balancing flavors and making your food more delicious.

1. Enhancing Flavors: Salt has the remarkable ability to bring out the best in ingredients. It heightens the natural taste of foods, making them more vibrant and enjoyable to eat.

2. Balancing Sweetness: Salt counteracts excessive sweetness in dishes, such as desserts or sauces, creating a perfect harmony of flavors.

3. Reducing Bitterness: In certain ingredients like leafy greens or eggplant, a pinch of salt can tone down bitterness, making them more palatable.

4. Boosting Savory Notes: Salt enhances savory flavors in meats, soups, and stews, turning ordinary dishes into mouthwatering feasts.

5. Tenderizing Meat: Salt can help break down proteins, making meat more tender and juicy.

6. Preserving Food: Historically, salt has been used as a method of preserving food, preventing spoilage and extending shelf life.

However, moderation is key. Too much salt can overpower the other flavors, so it's essential to taste as you cook and add salt gradually. By understanding the role of salt in cooking, you become the maestro of flavor, conducting a symphony of taste that leaves everyone wanting more. So, sprinkle, pinch, and season with confidence to elevate your culinary creations!

"Salt: A captivating culinary alchemist, magically transforming the ordinary into extraordinary with each delicate sprinkle."

Different Types of Salt and Their Uses

Salt comes in various forms, each with its unique characteristics and uses. Let's explore the different types of salt you might encounter in the kitchen:

1. Table Salt: This is the most common type of salt, finely ground and often containing additives like iodine for nutritional purposes. It's great for everyday cooking and seasoning dishes while providing a straightforward saltiness.

2. Kosher Salt: With a coarser texture and no additives, kosher salt is excellent for all-purpose seasoning and cooking. Its larger crystals make it easy to pinch and sprinkle, allowing for more precise control over the amount of salt added.

3. Sea Salt: Harvested from evaporated seawater, sea salt comes in various grain sizes and colors. It retains some natural minerals, lending a slightly different taste compared to table salt. It's perfect for both cooking and finishing dishes, adding a subtle briny flavor.

4. Himalayan Pink Salt: Mined from ancient sea beds in the Himalayan mountains, this salt has a pink hue due to trace minerals. It's often used as a finishing salt, adding a mild, earthy flavor to dishes.

5. Flaky Salt (e.g., Maldon): This type of salt has delicate, pyramid-shaped flakes, which add a delightful crunch and burst of flavor when sprinkled on top of finished dishes. It's commonly used for garnishing salads, roasted vegetables, and even desserts.

6. Rock Salt: Typically used for preserving and pickling, rock salt comes in large, coarse crystals.

It's also utilized in ice cream makers to lower the freezing temperature while making ice cream.

Remember, the type of salt you choose can impact the flavor, texture, and overall presentation of your dishes. So, have fun experimenting with different salts and discover how they can elevate your culinary creations! Happy seasoning and cooking!

Finding the Right Balance: Under-salting vs. Over-salting

Finding the right balance of salt in cooking is like walking a flavor tightrope – you want to avoid both under-salting and over-salting your dishes.

1. Under-Salting: When you under-salt, your food might taste dull and lackluster. The flavors won't pop, and the dish may feel flat and unexciting.

- **Solution:** Taste as you go and don't be afraid to add a pinch of salt at a time until the flavors come alive. Remember, you can always add more, but you can't take it back once it's in the pot.

2. Over-Salting: On the other hand, over-salting can overwhelm the other flavors in your dish, making it excessively salty and unpleasant to eat.

- **Solution:** If you accidentally over-salt, don't panic. Try diluting the dish by adding more unsalted ingredients or balancing the saltiness with sweetness or acidity. Lemon juice, vinegar, or a touch of sugar can help counteract excessive saltiness.
- **Preventive measures:** To avoid over-salting, it's best to start with less salt and gradually add more as needed. Keep in mind that certain ingredients (like salty sauces or cured meats)

can already contribute salt, so adjust accordingly.

- **Save the day:** If you find yourself with an over-salted dish, don't fret! You can try adding more ingredients to balance it out or serving it with plain rice or potatoes to absorb the excess salt.

With practice and tasting, you'll develop a sense of the right amount of salt to use, achieving that perfect balance that brings out the best flavors in your cooking.

So, walk that flavor tightrope confidently, and let your taste buds guide you to culinary excellence! Happy cooking!

Techniques for Salting

Dry Brining: Enhancing Flavors through Salting in Advance

Dry brining is like the flavor whisperer, enhancing the taste of your food through the magic of salting in advance. It's a simple technique that adds depth and juiciness to your meats and other ingredients.

How it works: Dry brining involves generously seasoning your food with salt and sometimes other spices or herbs, then letting it rest in the refrigerator for a few hours or even overnight. During this time, the salt slowly penetrates the food, drawing out moisture and then reabsorbing it, infusing the flavors and tenderizing the texture.

Benefits of Dry Brining:

1. Enhanced Flavor: Dry brining allows the salt to deeply permeate the food, enhancing its natural taste and bringing out its best flavors.

2. Juicy and Tender: The process of drawing out and reabsorbing moisture makes the food juicier and more tender.

3. Convenient: Unlike wet brining, which involves submerging food in a liquid solution, dry brining is less messy and requires less time and effort.

How to Dry Brine:

1. Choose your ingredients: Dry brining works wonders with meats like chicken, turkey, or pork, but it can also be used for vegetables or fish.

2. Season generously: Sprinkle a generous amount of salt all over the food, making sure to get it into every nook and cranny. You can add other herbs and spices to enhance the flavor further.

3. Refrigerate and wait: Place the seasoned food in the refrigerator, uncovered, to let the salt work its magic. The more it rests, the richer the flavors develop.

4. Cook as usual: After the recommended time, cook your dry-brined food as you normally would. You'll be delighted by the enhanced taste and tenderness.

So, the next time you want to take your cooking to the next level, try the flavor whisperer technique of dry brining. You'll be amazed at how this simple process can elevate your dishes and make your taste buds dance with joy. Happy dry brining and happy cooking!

Wet Brining: Moisture Retention and Seasoning Deep Dive

Imagine wet brining as a flavor-infusing spa treatment for your food! This technique keeps your meats juicy and packed with incredible taste.

How it works: Wet brining involves immersing your food, like turkey or chicken, in a saltwater bath. The salt penetrates the meat, attracting water and locking in moisture. This results in a tender and succulent dish.

Benefits of Wet Brining:

1. Juiciness: The brine's salt draws water into the meat, making it juicier and preventing it from drying out during cooking.

2. Flavor Boost: The saltwater solution acts like a taste conductor, infusing your food with incredible flavors, even deep into the meat.

3. Tender Texture: The salt breaks down proteins, softening the meat and making it melt in your mouth.

How to Wet Brine:

1. Prepare the Brine: In a large container, mix water with salt and other spices or herbs to create your flavorful bath.

2. Soak Your Food: Submerge your meat in the brine, ensuring it's fully covered. You can add some weight on top to keep it fully immersed.

3. Give It Time: Let your food bathe in the brine for a few hours or even overnight, allowing the magic to happen.

4. Rinse and Dry: Remove the food from the brine, give it a good rinse to remove excess salt, and pat it dry.

5. Cook to Perfection: Now, you can cook your wet-brined masterpiece, relishing the juicy and delicious results.

From Thanksgiving turkeys exquisitely tender to succulent chicken breasts bursting with flavor, wet brining ensures a mouthwatering and unforgettable culinary journey. So, pamper your taste buds with a spa-like treatment and immerse yourself in the delightful world of wet brining. Prepare to elevate your cooking to a whole new level of deliciousness.

Seasoning at Different Stages: Before, During, and After Cooking

Mastering the art of salting at different stages is like conducting a flavor symphony in your cooking. Knowing when to season before, during, or after cooking can make a world of difference in the taste of your dishes.

1. Before Cooking (Pre-Salting): Pre-salting is like laying the foundation for delicious flavors. Sprinkling salt on raw ingredients before cooking allows the salt to penetrate and enhance the natural taste.

- **For Meats:** Pre-salting tenderizes the proteins, improving texture and flavor. Let seasoned meat rest in the refrigerator for a while before cooking to achieve the best results.
- **For Vegetables:** Pre-salting draws out moisture, concentrating flavors, and enhancing their taste.

2. During Cooking: Salting during cooking is like fine-tuning the flavors as your dish comes together. This stage allows you to adjust the seasoning and ensure balanced taste.

- **Taste As You Go**: Regularly sample your dish during cooking, adding salt gradually until the flavors are just right.
- **Be Cautious With Salty Ingredients**: If your recipe includes ingredients like soy sauce, bacon, or cheese, be mindful of their saltiness and adjust your seasoning accordingly.

3. After Cooking (Post-Salting): Post-salting is like adding the final brushstroke to your masterpiece. This stage allows you to adjust the seasoning to perfection before serving.

- **Be Gentle**: Avoid over-salting at this stage; you can always add more, but it's difficult to undo excess salt.
- **For Salads and Cold Dishes**: Season right before serving, as salt can draw out moisture from vegetables, potentially making your dish watery.

Remember, seasoning at different stages is an essential skill that takes practice. Trust your taste buds, and don't be afraid to experiment with salt to achieve the perfect balance in your cooking. With time and experience, you'll become a salt maestro, creating delectable dishes that leave everyone craving for more. Happy seasoning and happy cooking!

Salt's Impact on Different Ingredients

Meats and Poultry

Salt's impact on meats and poultry is like a magical transformation, turning them into tender and flavorful delights. Let's dive into how salt works its wonders on these ingredients:

1. Tenderizing Effect: When you salt meats and poultry, the salt draws out some moisture, creating a concentrated brine. This brine is then reabsorbed, helping break down tough proteins and making the meat more tender.

2. Enhanced Flavor: Salt acts as a flavor enhancer, making the natural taste of meats and poultry shine. It elevates their savory notes, making every bite more enjoyable.

3. Juiciness: By helping retain moisture, salt ensures that your meats and poultry stay juicy and succulent, even after cooking.

Tips for Salting Meats and Poultry:

1. Pre-Salting: For thicker cuts of meat like roasts or whole chickens, pre-salting a few hours or even a day in advance can lead to more deeply infused flavors and better texture.

2. Even Distribution: Ensure the salt is evenly distributed over the entire surface of the meat or poultry for consistent seasoning.

3. Freshly Ground: If possible, use freshly ground salt for the best flavor impact.

4. Resting Time: After salting, let the meat rest for a while before cooking to allow the salt to work its magic.

5. Adjust to Taste: Taste as you go, and don't be afraid to add more salt if needed. Trust your taste buds to find the perfect balance.

Remember, salting is a skill that improves with practice. With a sprinkle of salt and a dash of know-how, you'll turn your meats and poultry into mouthwatering masterpieces that leave everyone wanting seconds.

Vegetables and Fruits

Salt's impact on vegetables and fruits is like adding a burst of flavor and enhancing their natural goodness. Let's explore how salt works its magic on these ingredients:

1. Flavor Enhancement: Salt brings out the best in vegetables and fruits by intensifying their taste. It heightens their inherent sweetness and savory notes, making them more enjoyable to eat.

2. Texture Improvement: When you sprinkle salt on vegetables, it draws out some moisture, concentrating their flavors and improving their texture.

3. Seasoning Balance: Salt is essential for achieving a well-balanced dish. It complements the natural flavors of vegetables and fruits, creating a harmonious taste.

Tips for Salting Vegetables and Fruits:

1. Even Sprinkling: Ensure the salt is evenly distributed over the vegetables or fruits for consistent seasoning.

2. Salting Time: For raw vegetables like cucumbers or tomatoes, sprinkle salt just before serving to maintain their crunchiness. For cooking, add salt during the process to enhance their flavors.

3. Taste Test: Taste as you go to avoid over-salting. Start with a small amount and adjust as needed.

4. Balancing Bitterness: Salt can help counteract the bitterness in certain vegetables like eggplants or leafy greens, making them more enjoyable.

5. Post-Cooking: For roasted or grilled vegetables, a light sprinkle of salt right after cooking can elevate their taste.

Remember, a little salt goes a long way. With a pinch of salt and some culinary finesse, you'll bring out the best in vegetables and fruits, creating delicious and vibrant dishes that celebrate the natural flavors

Pasta, Grains, and Legumes

Salt's impact on pasta, grains, and legumes is like adding a sprinkle of magic to these staple ingredients, elevating their taste and making them more delightful to savor. Let's delve into how salt works wonders with these kitchen essentials:

1. Flavor Enhancement: Salt brings out the inherent flavors of pasta, grains, and legumes, making them more delicious and satisfying.

2. Seasoning Throughout: When you add salt during cooking, it permeates the ingredients, ensuring a consistent and balanced taste.

3. Balancing Savory Notes: Salt complements the nutty and earthy flavors of grains and legumes, creating a harmonious taste.

4. Cooking Efficiency: Salt can enhance the cooking process by helping pasta and grains absorb water more efficiently, resulting in better texture and flavor.

Tips for Salting Pasta, Grains, and Legumes:

1. Salting Water: When boiling pasta or grains, add salt to the cooking water. It will season them from the inside out as they absorb the water.

2. Salt During Cooking: When preparing dishes like risotto or pilaf, add salt during the cooking process to infuse flavors evenly.

3. Taste Test: As with other ingredients, taste as you go and adjust the salt to your preference.

4. Avoid Over-Salting: Be mindful of other salty ingredients in your recipe, such as broth or canned beans, and adjust the salt accordingly.

5. Seasoning after Cooking: For certain dishes like salads or grain bowls, you can sprinkle a little salt over the finished dish to enhance the flavors.

With a pinch of salt, you can transform plain pasta, grains, and legumes into scrumptious and satisfying meals. It's a simple yet powerful way to make your everyday dishes shine. So, go ahead and sprinkle that magic touch, creating delightful culinary experiences with every bite.

Baked Goods and Desserts

Salt's impact on baked goods and desserts is like adding a dash of enchantment to these sweet creations. Let's explore how salt works its magic in these delightful treats:

1. Flavor Amplifier: Salt enhances the taste of baked goods and desserts, making their flavors pop and come alive.

2. Balancing Sweetness: In desserts, salt helps balance excessive sweetness, creating a harmonious taste that is not overly sugary.

3. Texture Booster: Salt contributes to the texture of baked goods, adding a subtle crunch and depth to cookies, brownies, and pie crusts.

4. Yeast Activation: In bread and other yeast-based desserts, salt activates yeast, helping the dough rise and giving a delightful flavor to the final product.

Tips for Salting Baked Goods and Desserts:

1. Follow the Recipe: When baking, it's essential to follow the recipe's salt measurements. Too much or too little salt can affect the taste and texture.

2. Use Fine Salt: For baking, use fine salt to ensure it dissolves evenly in the batter or dough.

3. Layering Flavors: In desserts with multiple components (e.g., cake with frosting), adding a pinch of salt to each layer enhances the overall flavor profile.

4. Taste and Adjust: Don't be afraid to taste the batter or dough before baking and adjust the salt if needed.

5. Finishing Touch: For some desserts, a light sprinkle of flaky salt on top just before serving adds an exciting burst of flavor.

From flaky pastries to gooey chocolate chip cookies, salt is the secret ingredient that elevates the taste and takes your baked goods and desserts to the next level. So, let the magic of salt bring joy to your sweet creations and create unforgettable experiences for your taste buds.

Chapter 2

The Art of Fat

The Significance of Fat in Cooking

Fat is like the culinary superstar in cooking, bringing richness, flavor, and texture to your dishes. Its significance lies in its ability to transform ordinary ingredients into extraordinary delights. Let's explore why fat plays a starring role in the kitchen:

1. Flavor Amplifier: Fat acts like a flavor carrier, enhancing the taste of your ingredients and making your dishes more delicious.

2. Mouthwatering Texture: In cooking, fat creates a luscious and velvety mouthfeel, making your food feel indulgent and satisfying.

"Fat: The brush that adds richness to every culinary masterpiece."

3. Heat Conduction: Fat is a champion when it comes to conducting heat, ensuring even cooking and preventing your food from sticking to the pan.

4. Browning Magic: When sautéing or roasting, fat aids in browning, adding beautiful colors and complex flavors to your creations.

5. Binding Agent: In baking, fat works as a binding agent, holding ingredients together and giving structure to cakes, cookies, and pastries.

6. Tenderizer: Fat helps break down proteins, making meats and other ingredients tender and juicy.

Understanding Different Types of Fats: Animal and Plant-Based

Understanding different types of fats is like unlocking the secrets to delicious and healthy cooking. Fats can be classified into two main categories: animal-based and plant-based. Let's explore each of them:

Animal-Based Fats:

- Butter: A creamy and flavorful fat made from milk, perfect for baking, sautéing, and adding richness to dishes.
- Lard: Rendered pork fat with a rich, savory taste, great for frying and creating flaky pie crusts.

- Bacon Fat: The flavorful leftover fat from cooking bacon, ideal for adding smoky goodness to various dishes.
- Duck Fat: A luxurious fat with a unique taste, perfect for roasting vegetables or frying potatoes.

2. Plant-Based Fats:

- Olive Oil: A heart-healthy oil with a fruity taste, excellent for salad dressings, sautéing, and roasting.
- Canola Oil: A versatile and neutral-flavored oil, suitable for high-heat cooking and baking.
- Avocado Oil: A rich and buttery oil, great for drizzling over salads or using in cooking.
- Coconut Oil: A tropical-flavored oil, solid at room temperature, ideal for baking and sautéing.

The Good and the Bad:

- Good Fats: Unsaturated fats, found in plant-based oils like olive oil and avocados, are heart-healthy and can help lower bad cholesterol levels.

- Bad Fats: Saturated fats, present in animal-based fats like butter and lard, can raise bad cholesterol levels and contribute to heart disease if consumed in excess.

Incorporating Healthy Fats:

- Choose plant-based oils and fats whenever possible to promote heart health.
- Use small amounts of animal-based fats for flavor enhancement, but avoid excessive consumption.

Remember, fats are essential for flavor, texture, and overall cooking success. By understanding the different types of fats and making conscious choices, you'll create delicious and nutritious meals that please both your taste buds and your health.

Choosing the Right Fat for Various Cooking Techniques

Choosing the right fat for various cooking techniques is like finding the perfect partner for a dance – it's all about complementing flavors and textures. Let's explore which fats shine in different cooking methods:

1. Sautéing and Frying:

- Butter: Adds rich and nutty flavors, perfect for sautéing vegetables, searing meats, and making pan sauces.
- Olive Oil: With its fruity taste, it's great for sautéing vegetables, frying, and even drizzling over finished dishes.

2. Baking:

- Butter: Provides a wonderful flavor and tender texture in baked goods like cookies, cakes, and pastries.
- Vegetable Oil: A versatile choice for baking, ensuring moist and tender results in cakes and muffins.

3. Roasting:

- Olive Oil: Its robust flavor brings out the best in roasted vegetables and meats.
- Duck Fat: Adds a luxurious touch, enhancing the taste of roasted potatoes and root vegetables.

4. Dressings and Marinades:

- Olive Oil: The classic choice for salad dressings and marinades, infusing dishes with its fruity taste.
- Avocado Oil: Perfect for creating creamy dressings and adding richness to marinades.

5. Deep Frying:

- Canola Oil: A neutral-flavored oil with a high smoke point, ideal for deep frying and stir-frying.

6. Flavor Enhancement:

- Bacon Fat: Adds smoky goodness to various dishes, elevating the taste with its unique flavor.
- Sesame Oil: Imparts a distinct nutty taste, perfect for drizzling over Asian-inspired dishes.

Remember, when choosing the right fat for your cooking techniques, consider the flavor you want to achieve, the cooking temperature, and the health implications. Moderation is key, and using a variety of fats can add excitement and depth to your culinary creations. So, let the fats do their dance in the kitchen, and enjoy the delicious results!

Techniques for Applying Fat

Searing: Enhancing Flavor and Texture

Searing is like creating a flavor-packed crust on your food, enhancing both its taste and texture. This technique is perfect for meats, poultry, and even some vegetables. Let's dive into how searing works its magic:

1. Flavor Enhancement: When you sear, the high heat caramelizes the surface of your food, creating a golden-brown crust. This crust is rich in savory flavors, adding a delightful depth to your dish.

2. Texture Transformation: Searing helps lock in the natural juices of the food, resulting in a tender and juicy interior, while the exterior becomes beautifully crispy.

Tips for Searing:

1. Dry Food Surface: Ensure your food's surface is dry before searing. Pat it dry with paper towels to promote better browning.

2. Preheat the Pan: Use a heavy-bottomed skillet or a cast-iron pan for even heat distribution. Preheat the pan over medium-high to high heat before adding the fat.

3. Use High Smoke Point Fat: Choose fats with a high smoke point, like vegetable oil or clarified butter (ghee), as they won't burn at high temperatures.

4. Don't Overcrowd: Sear in batches, leaving enough space between the food pieces. Overcrowding can release moisture, preventing proper browning.

5. Don't Flip Too Early: Allow the food to develop a crust on one side before flipping. This ensures the desired texture and flavor.

6. Resting: After searing, let the food rest for a few minutes before serving. This allows the juices to redistribute and makes the meat even more tender.

So, with a hot pan, sizzling fat, and a little patience, you'll achieve mouthwatering results through searing. The golden-brown crust and rich flavors will elevate your dishes to new heights, impressing everyone around the table.

Roasting: Basting and Pan Dripping

Roasting is like a slow and flavorful journey for your food, and basting and pan dripping are the secret ingredients that make it even more special. Let's explore these techniques and how they enhance your roasting experience:

1. Roasting: Roasting is a cooking method where food, often meats or vegetables, is cooked at a high temperature in the oven. This dry-heat cooking allows the ingredients to caramelize, resulting in rich flavors and appealing textures.

2. Basting: Basting is like giving your roasting ingredients a comforting hug. It involves periodically spooning or brushing melted fat, such as butter or oil, over the food while it cooks. Basting keeps the food moist and adds a lovely glaze to the surface.

- How to Baste: To baste, simply remove the roasting pan from the oven (while wearing oven mitts), tilt it slightly, and use a spoon or basting brush to drizzle the hot fat over the food. Then, return the pan to the oven to continue cooking.

3. Pan Dripping: Pan dripping is like collecting the essence of your roasted creation. It's the flavorful liquid that accumulates at the bottom of the roasting pan during cooking.

- How to Use Pan Dripping: After roasting, you can use the pan drippings to make a delicious sauce or gravy by adding some liquid (like broth or wine) and thickening it with flour or cornstarch. This sauce complements the roasted food beautifully.

Tips for Basting and Pan Dripping:

- Use a Basting Brush: A basting brush allows for even distribution of the fat and helps create a beautiful glaze on the food.
- Don't Overbaste: Baste sparingly to avoid lowering the oven temperature too much, as this can prolong the cooking time.
- Deglaze the Pan: To capture all the flavors from the roasting process, deglaze the pan by adding liquid (like broth or wine) and scraping up the browned bits with a wooden spoon. This adds depth to your sauce.

Roasting, basting, and pan dripping are a trifecta of flavor-boosting techniques that make your dishes truly extraordinary. So, embrace these techniques, and let the oven work its magic on your next roasting adventure.

Sauteing and Stir-Frying: Achieving Even Coating and Heat Distribution

Sauteing and stir-frying are like high-energy cooking dances that require even coating and sizzling heat distribution. Let's uncover these techniques and how to achieve culinary perfection:

1. Sauteing: Sauteing involves cooking food quickly in a hot pan with a small amount of fat. The goal is to create beautifully browned and tender results.

2. Stir-Frying: Stir-frying is a speedy Asian cooking technique where ingredients are constantly stirred and tossed in a hot wok or pan with a small amount of oil. The quick cooking retains vibrant colors and crisp textures.

Techniques for Even Coating and Heat Distribution:

1. Preheat the Pan: For both sauteing and stir-frying, preheat the pan over medium-high to high heat until it's hot. This ensures even heat distribution and prevents sticking.

2. Use the Right Fat: Choose fats with high smoke points like vegetable oil or peanut oil, suitable for the high temperatures of sauteing and stir-frying.

3. Add Fat Gradually: Start with a small amount of fat in the pan. You can add more as needed during cooking if the ingredients begin to stick.

4. Coat Ingredients Evenly: For sauteing, ensure the ingredients are spread in a single layer, allowing them to cook evenly. For stir-frying, keep the ingredients moving constantly for uniform cooking.

5. Cook in Batches: When stir-frying, cook ingredients in batches to avoid overcrowding the pan, ensuring proper browning and quick cooking.

6. Constantly Stir: Keep the food moving in the pan during stir-frying to prevent sticking and ensure consistent heat distribution.

7. Don't Overcook: Both sauteing and stir-frying are quick cooking methods, so be vigilant to avoid overcooking and maintain the desired textures.

With these techniques, you'll master the art of sauteing and stir-frying, achieving even coating of flavors and sizzling heat distribution. So, toss, stir, and savor the delicious results of your culinary dance! Happy sauteing, happy stir-frying, and happy cooking!

Balancing Flavors with Fat

Using Fat to Tame Acidity and Bitterness

Balancing flavors with fat is like creating a delicious harmony in your dishes, and it can be especially helpful in taming acidity and bitterness. Here's how fat comes to the rescue:

1. Taming Acidity: When a dish has a tangy or acidic taste, adding a touch of fat can soften and balance the flavors. Fat coats the taste buds, reducing the sharpness of the acidity and creating a more rounded and pleasing sensation on the palate.

2. Countering Bitterness: Bitterness can be off-putting in some dishes, but fat can work wonders in neutralizing it. Fat adds a rich and smooth texture that helps counteract the bitter taste, making the dish more enjoyable.

Tips for Balancing Flavors with Fat:

1. Creamy Sauces: When making sauces with acidic ingredients like tomatoes or citrus, consider adding a dollop of butter, cream, or olive oil. This will mellow out the acidity and create a luxurious texture.

2. Dressings and Vinaigrettes: In salads or dressings that have a tangy kick, use an oil-based dressing to balance the acidity. The fat will complement the acidity, making the dressing more well-rounded and satisfying.

3. Bitter Greens: For dishes with bitter greens like kale or arugula, toss them with a drizzle of olive oil or a sprinkle of grated cheese. The fat will help mellow the bitterness and enhance the overall taste.

4. Creamy Beverages: In beverages like coffee or hot chocolate that can be bitter, adding a splash of cream or milk can bring a velvety richness that offsets the bitterness.

Remember, balance is the key to culinary perfection, and using fat to tame acidity and bitterness is a smart technique. Embrace the magical touch of fat in your cooking, and your dishes will sing with delightful flavors.

Incorporating Fat for Richness and Creaminess

Crichness and creaminess that elevates the taste to new heights. Here's how fat brings this delightful experience to your cooking:

1. Richness: Fat contributes luxurious and velvety textures to your dishes, making them more indulgent and satisfying. It coats the palate, leaving a smooth and delightful sensation with each bite.

2. Creaminess: Adding fat to recipes creates a creamy mouthfeel that enhances the overall eating experience. It brings a luscious quality that makes dishes feel comforting and irresistible.

Tips for Incorporating Fat for Richness and Creaminess:

1. Sauces and Gravies: When making sauces or gravies, whisk in butter or cream at the end to add a luxurious richness that brings the dish together.

2. Soups and Stews: For heartwarming soups and stews, stir in a dollop of heavy cream or coconut milk to achieve a silky and creamy texture.

3. Mashed Potatoes: When making mashed potatoes, add a generous amount of butter or olive oil to achieve that heavenly creamy consistency.

4. Creamy Desserts: In desserts like custards or puddings, the addition of egg yolks, cream, or melted chocolate creates a dreamy creaminess that delights the senses.

5. Creamy Dressings: For salad dressings, whisk together oils and mayonnaise or yogurt to create creamy and flavorful dressings that coat the greens beautifully.

Remember, incorporating fat for richness and creaminess is like an invitation to savor the most indulgent culinary experiences. It's about finding the right balance and using fat as a tool to enhance the flavors and textures of your dishes. So, embrace the creaminess, indulge in the richness, and let your taste buds dance with delight.

Achieving Crispness with the Right Amount of Fat

Balancing flavors with fat is like finding the perfect rhythm in your cooking, and it can also help you achieve that coveted crispness in your dishes. Here's how to strike the right balance with fat for crisp and delightful results:

1. Crispness and Fat: Fat plays a crucial role in achieving crisp textures in various foods. When heated, fat creates a golden and crunchy exterior while keeping the inside tender and moist.

2. Deep-Frying: Deep-frying involves submerging food in hot oil, creating a crispy and delicious outer layer. The oil surrounds the food, ensuring even heat distribution for that satisfying crunch.

3. Pan-Frying: Pan-frying uses a smaller amount of fat compared to deep-frying, but it's enough to achieve a crispy texture on the surface of the food.

4. Roasting: When roasting vegetables or meats, brushing them with a thin layer of oil allows the surface to crisp up, resulting in delectable textures.

Tips for Achieving Crispness with the Right Amount of Fat:

1. Use the Right Oil: Choose oils with high smoke points, like vegetable oil, canola oil, or peanut oil, for frying and roasting. They can withstand the high temperatures needed for achieving crispness.

2. Don't Overcrowd: Whether you're deep-frying or pan-frying, avoid overcrowding the pan. Cook in batches if needed to ensure that each piece has enough space to become crispy.

3. Blot Excess Fat: After frying, blot excess oil on paper towels to avoid an overly greasy texture while still maintaining crispness.

4. Roast with Care: When roasting, toss the ingredients with just enough oil to coat them evenly. Too much oil can lead to soggy results instead of the desired crispiness.

5. Embrace Seasonings: Enhance the crispy experience by adding seasoning to the fat or coating the food before frying or roasting. Spices, herbs, and even a touch of salt can take your dish to the next level.

Balancing flavors with fat and achieving crispness go hand in hand to create culinary perfection. Master the art of using the right amount of fat, and your dishes will boast that desirable crunch while being irresistibly delicious.

Note

Chapter 3

Mastering Acid

The Versatility of Acid in Cooking

The versatility of acid in cooking is like having a secret weapon that can transform your dishes from dull to delightful. Acid adds brightness, balance, and depth to a wide range of foods. Let's explore its superpowers:

1. Flavor Enhancer: Acid acts like a magic enhancer, making other flavors in your dish pop. It brings out the natural taste of ingredients, creating a more vibrant and satisfying eating experience.

2. Balancing Act: Acid is a master at balancing flavors. It can tame excessive sweetness, counteract richness, and even mellow out excessive bitterness.

3. Tenderizer: In certain dishes, acid works as a tenderizer, breaking down proteins in meat or vegetables and making them more tender and succulent.

4. Marinades and Dressings: Acid is a star player in marinades and dressings, infusing dishes with zesty and tangy goodness.

5. Preservative: Acid can also act as a natural preservative, helping to extend the shelf life of pickled foods and preventing the browning of fruits and vegetables.

Common Acids Used in Cooking:

"Mastering acid adds a vibrant melody to your dishes, awakening flavors and leaving a lingering symphony on your palate."

- **Citrus Fruits:** Lemon, lime, orange, and grapefruit are commonly used to add a refreshing tang to dishes.

- **Vinegars:** Different types of vinegar, like balsamic, apple cider, and rice vinegar, bring diverse flavors to recipes.

- **Yogurt:** This dairy product contains lactic acid, providing a tangy taste in marinades and sauces.

Tips for Using Acid:

- Balance is Key: Use acid judiciously to achieve the right balance of flavors without overpowering the dish.
- Taste as You Go: Add acid gradually and taste as you cook to get the desired level of tanginess.
- Experiment with Pairings: Try different combinations of acid with various ingredients to discover exciting flavor profiles.

Acid's versatility in cooking is undeniable, and with a splash of citrus or a dash of vinegar, you can elevate your dishes to new heights of deliciousness. Embrace the power of acid, and let it be your culinary sidekick in creating flavorful and captivating meals.

Identifying Various Acids: Citrus, Vinegar, and Beyond

Identifying various acids in cooking is like recognizing the stars of the flavor show. Let's meet the main characters, including citrus fruits, vinegar, and some lesser-known heroes:

1. Citrus Fruits: Citrus fruits are the bright and zesty rockstars of the acid world. They include lemons, limes, oranges, grapefruits, and more. These juicy wonders add a refreshing tanginess to dishes, elevating both sweet and savory recipes.

2. Vinegar: Vinegar is the versatile and dependable companion in cooking. It comes in various types, such as balsamic, apple cider, red wine, white wine, and rice vinegar. Each variety brings its unique flavor profile, from fruity and sweet to tangy and sharp.

3. Yogurt: This creamy acid hero contains lactic acid, providing a gentle tang to marinades, dressings, and sauces. It also adds a velvety texture to dishes.

4. Buttermilk: Another dairy delight, buttermilk is a cultured acid that imparts a mild tang to baked goods and marinades while adding moisture and tenderness.

5. Fermented Foods: Foods like kimchi, sauerkraut, and pickles owe their tangy goodness to natural fermentation, which produces beneficial acids.

6. Tomatoes: Tomatoes are a culinary powerhouse, containing citric and malic acids that add depth to sauces and dishes.

7. Wine: Wine not only brings depth and richness to cooking but also introduces tartness when reduced in sauces and stews.

Identifying these various acids is like having a flavorful palette at your disposal. Each acid brings its unique charm, and learning to use them can turn your cooking into a symphony of taste.

So, embrace these culinary stars, mix and match, and let the tangy adventures begin! Happy cooking and happy acid exploration!

Balancing Flavors with Acid: Sourness vs. Sweetness

Balancing flavors with acid is like finding the perfect dance partner for your taste buds. When it comes to sourness and sweetness, they are like two sides of a delicious coin. Let's explore how acid plays a pivotal role in achieving harmony between these flavors:

1. Sourness: Sourness is the tangy and zesty flavor that acid brings to a dish. It can come from various sources like citrus fruits, vinegar, and fermented foods. Sourness adds brightness and excitement, awakening the palate with its refreshing taste.

2. Sweetness: Sweetness is the delightful taste of sugar and other natural sweeteners present in ingredients like fruits, honey, and syrups. It brings a pleasant and comforting sensation, satisfying our sweet cravings.

Balancing Act with Acid:

1. Taming Sweetness: When a dish is too sweet, adding a touch of acid can work wonders. The acid cuts through the sweetness, creating a more balanced and complex taste.

2. Enhancing Sweetness: On the other hand, a hint of acid can enhance the sweetness in certain dishes. It brightens the natural sweetness of fruits and other ingredients, making them shine even more.

3. Sauces and Dressings: In sauces and dressings, a well-balanced combination of sourness and sweetness can take your dish to the next level.

4. Marinades and Glazes: When marinating or glazing meats and vegetables, the interplay of acid, sourness, and sweetness creates a delightful depth of flavor.

Tips for Balancing Flavors:

- Start with a little acid and sweetener, and taste as you go. Adjust the balance until you achieve the desired harmony.
- Citrus fruits and vinegar are excellent options for balancing flavors, offering a range of sourness to suit different dishes.
- Experiment with various combinations to find the perfect match for your taste preferences.

In the culinary world, balancing flavors with acid is like performing a flavorful dance. Embrace the interplay of sourness and sweetness, and you'll create dishes that are both bright and comforting, leaving your taste buds delighted with every bite.

Techniques for Incorporating Acid

Marinating: Tenderizing and Flavoring with Acid

Marinating is like giving your ingredients a delightful spa treatment, tenderizing and infusing them with flavorful goodness. Using acid in marinades is a powerful technique that works wonders in transforming your dishes. Let's explore how marinating with acid can elevate your cooking:

1. Tenderizing Power: Acid, such as citrus juice or vinegar, acts as a natural tenderizer. It breaks down proteins in meats and other ingredients, making them more tender and juicy when cooked.

2. Flavor Infusion: Marinating with acid allows the flavors to penetrate deep into the food.

As the acid soaks in, it imparts a tangy and zesty taste, enhancing the overall flavor profile of the dish.

Techniques for Successful Marinating with Acid:

1. Choose the Right Acid: Citrus fruits like lemon, lime, and orange, as well as vinegar, work well as marinating acids. Select the one that complements the flavors of your dish.

2. Balance the Flavors: Combine the acid with other ingredients like oil, herbs, spices, and sweeteners to create a balanced and delicious marinade.

3. Marinating Time: The marinating time varies depending on the type of meat or ingredient. Delicate

The Salt Fat Acid Cookbook for Beginners

seafood may need only a short marinating time, while tougher cuts of meat benefit from longer marination.

4. Refrigeration: Always marinate in the refrigerator to keep the food safe from bacteria growth.

5. Avoid Over-Marinating: Be cautious not to marinate for too long, especially with strong acids like vinegar, as it can start to break down the food excessively.

Tips for Perfect Marinating:

- Use a resealable plastic bag or a shallow dish to evenly coat the food with the marinade.
- If you plan to use the marinade as a sauce or glaze, reserve a portion before adding the raw ingredients to avoid contamination.
- Pat the food dry before cooking to ensure proper browning and prevent excessive moisture during cooking.

Marinating with acid is a culinary journey that transforms ordinary ingredients into tender and flavor-packed delights. Embrace the power of acid,

Page **67** of **162**

and let your marinated creations shine with succulence and taste.

Finishing Dishes with a Touch of Acid

Finishing dishes with a touch of acid is like adding a dazzling final flourish to your culinary masterpiece. It's a simple yet powerful technique that can elevate the flavors of your dishes. Let's uncover how this little touch of acid can make a big difference:

1. Enhancing Flavors: Adding a small amount of acid, such as a squeeze of lemon juice or a splash of vinegar, at the end of cooking enhances the overall taste of the dish. The acid brightens the flavors and brings a refreshing zing to your creation.

2. Balancing Act: Acid works as a natural balancer, harmonizing the different elements in your dish. It can tame excessive richness or sweetness, making the flavors more well-rounded and satisfying.

3. Crisp and Clean Finish: The acidity in the finishing touch leaves a clean and crisp sensation on the palate, making your dish feel lighter and more enjoyable.

4. Versatility: From savory to sweet dishes, finishing with acid is a versatile technique that complements a wide range of cuisines and ingredients.

Simple Tips for Finishing with Acid:

- **Taste and Adjust:** Add the acid gradually and taste as you go to achieve the desired level of brightness without overwhelming the dish.
- **Citrus or Vinegar:** Lemon, lime, orange, or different types of vinegar are excellent choices for finishing with acid, each offering its unique character.
- **Drizzle or Sprinkle:** Depending on the dish, you can drizzle the acid over the top or lightly sprinkle it to evenly distribute the flavor.
- **Experiment and Explore:** Don't be afraid to experiment with different types of acid and discover the exciting possibilities they bring to your dishes.

The art of finishing with a touch of acid is like the final brushstroke on a beautiful painting, adding depth and brilliance to your culinary creations. Embrace this technique, and your dishes will shine with vibrant flavors and an unforgettable finishing touch

Pickling and Fermentation: Preserving and Transforming Ingredients

Pickling and fermentation are like time-traveling techniques that preserve and transform ingredients into flavorful delights. Let's dive into these magical processes and how they work their wonders:

1. Pickling: Pickling involves preserving ingredients by immersing them in a mixture of acid, usually vinegar, along with salt, sugar, and spices. This acidic environment preserves the ingredients, keeping them fresh and flavorful for a long time.

- **Quick Pickling:** In quick pickling, ingredients are soaked in a vinegar solution for a short time, usually a few hours or overnight. This process imparts a tangy taste and adds a burst of flavor to the ingredients.
- **Canning:** Canning is a heat-based pickling method where jars filled with acid and ingredients are heated to create airtight seals, extending their shelf life.

2. Fermentation: Fermentation is a natural preservation process where microorganisms, like bacteria or yeast, convert sugars into acid and alcohol. This process not only preserves the ingredients but also enhances their flavors and nutritional value.

- Lacto-Fermentation: This type of fermentation uses beneficial bacteria to produce lactic acid, creating tangy and probiotic-rich foods like sauerkraut, kimchi, and pickles.
- Alcoholic Fermentation: In this process, yeast converts sugars into alcohol, which is then used in brewing and making alcoholic beverages.

Benefits of Pickling and Fermentation:

- Flavor Transformation: Pickling and fermentation turn ordinary ingredients into complex, tangy, and delicious creations.
- Preservation: These techniques extend the shelf life of ingredients, allowing you to enjoy seasonal flavors all year round.

- Probiotic Boost: Fermented foods are rich in probiotics, promoting a healthy gut and aiding digestion.
- Unique Ingredients: The pickling and fermentation process allows you to experiment with unique flavor combinations, creating one-of-a-kind dishes.

Tips for Pickling and Fermentation:

- Use Clean Equipment: Ensure all equipment and containers are clean and free of contaminants to avoid spoilage.
- Be Patient: Both processes take time to develop flavors. Let the ingredients sit and ferment at their own pace.
- Experiment with Spices: Play around with different spices and herbs to create unique flavor profiles.

Pickling and fermentation are ancient techniques that not only preserve ingredients but also unlock new depths of flavor. Embrace the magic of these processes in your kitchen, and your dishes will transform into delectable delights that delight your taste buds.

The Impact of Acid on Different Ingredients

Seafood and Fish

The impact of acid on seafood and fish is like unlocking a treasure trove of flavors, enhancing the taste and texture of these ocean delights. Let's dive into how acid works its magic on seafood:

1. Flavor Enhancement: Acid, such as lemon or lime juice, brightens the natural flavors of seafood and fish, making them taste fresher and more vibrant.

2. Balance and Complexity: Acid balances the richness of seafood, especially in dishes like creamy chowders or buttery sauces, creating a harmonious and well-rounded taste.

3. Ceviche and Marinades: Acid is a star player in ceviche and marinades. When raw seafood is marinated in citrus juices, the acid "cooks" the fish, giving it a tender texture and infusing it with delightful tangy flavors.

4. Complementing Sauces: Acid in sauces, like a squeeze of lemon over grilled fish, adds a tantalizing finishing touch, elevating the dish to new heights.

Tips for Using Acid with Seafood and Fish:

- Choose the Right Acid: Citrus fruits like lemon, lime, and orange are popular choices for seafood. Vinegar can also be used in some dishes.

- Balance the Amount: Use acid judiciously to avoid overpowering the delicate flavors of seafood. A little goes a long way.

- Timing Matters: For ceviche or marinated dishes, let the seafood sit in the acid for just the right amount of time to achieve the desired texture and flavor.

- Season with Care: Balance the acid with other seasonings like salt, pepper, and herbs to create a well-rounded taste.

- Freshness is Key: Acid works best with fresh seafood, enhancing its natural taste and aroma.

The impact of acid on seafood and fish is truly transformative, taking your culinary creations to the next level. Embrace the zesty power of acid in your seafood dishes, and you'll be rewarded with delicious and delightful results that will leave your taste buds swimming in joy.

Greens and Salads

The impact of acid on greens and salads is like adding a burst of freshness and excitement to your plate. Let's explore how acid works its magic on these leafy delights:

1. Brightens the Flavors: Acid, like lemon juice or vinegar, brightens the natural flavors of greens, making them taste more vibrant and alive.

2. Balances the Taste: Acid helps balance the bitterness of some greens, creating a harmonious taste that is refreshing and enjoyable.

3. Enhances Dressings: Acid is a key ingredient in salad dressings, providing a tangy and zesty kick that ties all the flavors together.

4. Crispens Greens: Acid helps crisp up the texture of greens, making them more appealing to the palate.

Tips for Using Acid in Greens and Salads:

- Choose the Right Acid: Citrus fruits like lemon, lime, or orange, as well as various types of vinegar, work well with greens.

- Dress with Care: When making salad dressings, start with a small amount of acid and taste as you go to achieve the desired level of tanginess.

- Mix and Match: Experiment with different acid options to discover unique flavor combinations that complement the greens in your salad.

- Use Fresh Ingredients: For the best results, use fresh greens and dress them with acid just before serving to preserve their crispness and flavors.

- Avoid Overdressing: Add the acid gradually to avoid overdressing the salad, which can overpower the other ingredients.

The impact of acid on greens and salads is like a delightful wake-up call for your taste buds. Embrace the zesty goodness of acid, and your salads will become a refreshing and irresistible highlight of any meal.

Dairy and Cheese

The impact of acid on dairy and cheese is like a culinary magic trick that transforms textures and enhances flavors. Let's discover how acid works its wonders in the world of dairy:

1. Coagulation and Curdling: Acid plays a crucial role in coagulating milk proteins, leading to curdling.

This process is essential in cheese-making, where acid helps form the curds that eventually become cheese.

2. Flavor Enhancement: When acid is added to dairy products like yogurt or sour cream, it imparts a tangy taste that elevates the overall flavor profile.

3. Tenderizing and Marinating: Acid can be used to tenderize certain types of cheese, and it is also utilized in marinating feta and other cheeses to infuse them with delightful tanginess.

4. Cheese-Making: In the cheese-making process, specific acids, like citric acid or lemon juice, are often used to curdle the milk, creating various types of cheese with distinct textures and flavors.

Tips for Using Acid with Dairy and Cheese:

- **Balance the Amount:** Use acid judiciously, especially when adding it to dairy products, to avoid overwhelming the flavors.
- **Cheese Selection:** Choose the right type of cheese for your dish, considering the acidity level of the cheese and how it complements other ingredients.
- **Experiment with Flavors:** Add a splash of acid to yogurt, sour cream, or cream cheese to experiment with new taste sensations.
- **Cheese Preservation:** In some recipes, acid can be used to preserve cheese or prevent it from spoiling.

The impact of acid on dairy and cheese is a delicious alchemy that adds complexity and excitement to these dairy delights. Whether it's making cheese from scratch or enhancing the flavors of dairy-based dishes, acid brings a refreshing twist to the world of dairy. Embrace this magical culinary trick, and your dairy creations will shine with newfound zest and appeal.

Desserts and Sweets

The impact of acid on desserts and sweets is like adding a spark of excitement and balance to your sweet creations. Let's explore how acid works its magic in the world of desserts:

1. Brightens Flavors: Acid, such as citrus juice or vinegar, brightens the flavors of desserts, making them taste more lively and refreshing.

2. Balances Sweetness: Acid is a perfect counterbalance to excessive sweetness in desserts, creating a harmonious taste that is not overwhelmingly sugary.

3. Enhances Fruit Flavors: When added to fruit-based desserts, acid brings out the natural sweetness and tanginess of the fruits, making them even more delectable.

4. Adds Complexity: Acid adds a layer of complexity to desserts, elevating their taste from simple to extraordinary.

5. Sets Puddings and Jellies: Acid, like lemon juice, is used in making desserts like lemon curd and panna cotta, where it helps to set and firm the texture.

Tips for Using Acid in Desserts and Sweets:

- **Choose the Right Acid:** Citrus fruits like lemon, lime, and orange, as well as various types of vinegar, work well in desserts. Select the one that complements the flavors of your sweet treats.

- **Balance the Amount:** Use acid judiciously to achieve the desired level of tanginess without overpowering the sweetness.

- **Experiment with Pairings:** Try different acid options with various desserts to discover unique and delightful flavor combinations.

- **Add a Finishing Touch:** A drizzle of lemon juice or a splash of vinegar can be the perfect finishing touch to brighten up your dessert.

The impact of acid on desserts and sweets is like a magical touch that transforms ordinary treats into extraordinary delights. Embrace the zesty goodness of acid in your sweet creations, and your desserts will leave a lasting impression on every dessert lover's taste buds.

Chapter 4

Mastering Heat

Understanding the Power of Heat

Understanding the power of heat is like unraveling the secret to cooking's transformative magic. Heat is the key that turns raw ingredients into delicious meals. Let's explore its power:

1. Cooking Magic: Heat changes the texture, flavor, and appearance of food. It's the wizardry that makes ingredients tender, crispy, and mouthwateringly tasty.

2. Energy Transfer: Heat moves from the heat source to the food through conduction, convection, or radiation, cooking it from the outside in or vice versa.

"Within the kitchen's embrace, we wield the alchemical power of heat, turning raw ingredients into culinary poetry."

3. Maillard Reaction: The magic of heat creates the Maillard reaction, browning the surface of food, producing delicious flavors, and enhancing visual appeal.

4. Temperature Control: Understanding heat levels - low, medium, and high - gives you the power to control cooking speed and prevent overcooking or undercooking.

5. Versatility: Heat comes from various sources like ovens, stovetops, grills, and more, each offering unique cooking techniques and possibilities.

Tips for Mastering the Power of Heat:

- **Preheat Properly:** Allow your cooking surface or oven to reach the desired temperature before adding food for even cooking.
- **Timing Matters:** Keep an eye on cooking times to achieve perfect results and prevent burning or drying out.
- **Rest and Carryover Cooking:** Let cooked food rest before serving, as it continues to cook slightly, ensuring optimal tenderness and flavor.
- **Experiment:** Play with different heat levels and cooking methods to discover your culinary flair and create mouthwatering masterpieces.

Heat is the enchanting force that turns ingredients into culinary wonders. Embrace the power of heat, and you'll unlock the potential to create delicious, satisfying meals that will leave everyone spellbound.

Different Heat Sources: Oven, Stovetop, Grill, and More

Different heat sources in cooking are like a diverse cast of characters that bring unique flavors and textures to your dishes. Let's meet these culinary stars and discover how they work their magic:

1. Oven: The oven is like a gentle giant that surrounds your food with dry, even heat. It's perfect for baking, roasting meats and vegetables, and creating tender casseroles and desserts.

2. Stovetop: The stovetop is the versatile multitasker that offers various heat levels. It's great for sautéing, stir-frying, simmering soups, and making sauces.

3. Grill: The grill is the outdoor adventurer that imparts a smoky and charred flavor to your foods. It's excellent for grilling meats, vegetables, and even fruits, adding a delightful outdoor touch to your meals.

4. Broiler: The broiler is the quick and intense star that brings rapid high heat from above.

It's perfect for quickly browning and caramelizing the tops of dishes like casseroles and desserts.

5. Slow Cooker: The slow cooker is like the patient nurturer that gently cooks food over several hours. It's ideal for braising tough cuts of meat, creating tender and flavorful dishes.

6. Microwave: The microwave is the speedy assistant that quickly heats and reheats dishes, saving you time in the kitchen.

7. Sous Vide: The sous vide is the precision performer that cooks food in a water bath at a controlled temperature, delivering consistent and perfectly cooked results.

Tips for Using Different Heat Sources:

- **Match the Technique:** Choose the right heat source that aligns with the cooking technique you want to use.
- **Preheat Properly:** Preheat your oven or grill to ensure even and consistent cooking.

- **Time Management:** Plan your cooking time based on the heat source to ensure dishes are ready to serve when needed.
- **Experiment and Explore:** Try different heat sources to discover new flavors and textures in your dishes.

Embrace the diversity of heat sources in your kitchen, and you'll have a star-studded culinary journey. Each heat source has its unique charm, and mastering their techniques will elevate your cooking to new heights.

Heat Levels: Low, Medium, High, and Indirect Heat

Heat levels in cooking are like the volume controls for your culinary performance, determining how intensely the heat works its magic. Let's explore these heat levels and how they can transform your dishes:

1. Low Heat: Low heat is like a gentle caress, perfect for delicate tasks like simmering sauces, melting chocolate, and slow-cooking tough cuts of meat. It keeps your ingredients cooking slowly and evenly without scorching.

2. Medium Heat: Medium heat is the workhorse of the kitchen, providing steady and moderate heat. It's great for sautéing vegetables, searing meats, and cooking grains. This level ensures thorough cooking without burning.

3. High Heat: High heat is like a burst of energy, perfect for quick cooking and creating bold flavors. It's ideal for stir-frying, searing steaks, and achieving that beautiful caramelization on vegetables.

4. Indirect Heat: Indirect heat is like a patient and even-tempered teacher, used in grilling or barbecuing. It involves cooking food away from the direct flames, allowing it to cook slowly and evenly without charring.

Tips for Mastering Heat Levels:

- **Use the Right Tool:** Choose the appropriate burner or setting on your stovetop to control the heat level.
- **Adjust as Needed:** Be ready to adjust the heat level during cooking to maintain control and prevent overcooking or burning.

- **Practice and Observe:** Get to know your stovetop or grill's heat levels through practice and observation to become a heat master.
- **Use Timers:** Keep an eye on cooking times to ensure your dishes are cooked to perfection.

Playing with heat levels is like conducting a symphony of flavors in your kitchen. Each heat level brings its unique role, creating a harmonious and delicious culinary performance. Embrace the power of heat control, and you'll orchestrate incredible dishes that will leave your taste buds applauding.

Techniques for Controlling and Applying Heat

Braising and Stewing: Slow Cooking for Tenderness

Braising and stewing are like the gentle hugs of heat that transform tough ingredients into tender and flavorful wonders. Let's dive into these slow-cooking techniques and uncover their magic:

1. Braising: Braising is like a relaxing spa treatment for meat and vegetables. It involves searing the ingredient in a hot pan to lock in flavors, then simmering it in liquid over low heat for an extended period. This gentle and moist cooking method breaks down tough fibers, resulting in fork-tender and succulent dishes.

- **Perfect for Tough Cuts:** Braising works wonders with tougher cuts of meat, like beef chuck or lamb shanks, turning them into melt-in-your-mouth delicacies.
- **Flavorful Liquid:** The liquid used for braising, such as broth, wine, or tomatoes, infuses the ingredient with rich flavors, creating a luscious sauce to accompany the dish.

2. Stewing: Stewing is like a warm and comforting hug from a loved one. It involves cutting ingredients into bite-sized pieces and cooking them in liquid over low heat for an extended time. This slow-cooking method allows the flavors to meld, resulting in hearty and soul-soothing dishes.

- **Homely Comfort:** Stews are perfect for creating heartwarming dishes, like beef stew or chicken casserole, which comfort and satisfy with every spoonful.

- **Full Flavor Development:** The long and slow cooking process allows all the ingredients to release their flavors into the liquid, creating a harmonious and flavorful dish.

Tips for Braising and Stewing:

- **Patience is Key:** These techniques require patience, as the slow cooking time is crucial for achieving tender and flavorful results.
- **Season Well:** Be generous with seasonings to ensure your dish is bursting with deliciousness.
- **Select the Right Liquid:** Choose liquids that complement the dish, like broth for savory stews or wine for richer braises.
- **Low and Slow:** Keep the heat low throughout the cooking process to maintain the gentle simmer that gives the best results.

Braising and stewing are the culinary equivalent of a warm embrace, turning humble ingredients into extraordinary delights. Embrace the slow-cooking magic of these techniques, and your dishes will be filled with tenderness and flavor that will warm the hearts of all who taste them.

Grilling and Broiling: Intense Heat for Char and Flavor

Grilling and broiling are like the fiery performers of the culinary stage, adding a burst of intense heat that brings out charred and smoky flavors in your dishes. Let's uncover the secrets of these sizzling techniques:

1. Grilling: Grilling is like a backyard barbecue party with a sizzling grill as the star attraction. It involves cooking food directly over an open flame or hot coals, creating beautiful grill marks and a hint of smokiness.

- **Charred Goodness:** Grilling imparts a delightful charred flavor on the surface of meats, vegetables, and even fruits, adding a tempting smokiness to your dishes.
- **Quick and Intense:** Grilling is a fast and intense cooking method, perfect for tender cuts of meat and vegetables that cook quickly.

2. Broiling: Broiling is like a sun-kissed moment under a hot oven element. It involves cooking food directly under intense heat, similar to grilling, but without the need for an outdoor setup.

- Top-Down Magic: Broiling is a top-down cooking method, perfect for quickly browning the tops of dishes like casseroles or melting cheese on sandwiches.
- Rapid Cooking: Broiling cooks food quickly, making it ideal for achieving golden crusts and delicious caramelization.

Tips for Grilling and Broiling:

- Preheat and Oil: Preheat your grill or broiler and lightly oil the grates or pan to prevent sticking.
- High Heat: Both grilling and broiling require high heat to create those beautiful grill marks or the golden crust.
- Keep a Watchful Eye: These intense cooking methods can quickly go from perfectly cooked to overdone, so keep a close eye on your food.
- Marinades and Seasonings: Enhance the flavors of your ingredients with marinades and

seasonings before grilling or broiling for even more deliciousness.

Grilling and broiling are the dynamic duo that add exciting char and flavor to your dishes. Embrace the intense heat of these techniques, and your culinary creations will be a sizzling success that ignites taste buds and leaves everyone craving for more.

Steaming and Boiling: Preserving Nutrients and Texture

Steaming and boiling are like the gentle guardians of nutrients and textures, preserving the goodness of ingredients in a moist and loving environment. Let's explore these cooking techniques and how they work their magic:

1. Steaming: Steaming is like a cozy embrace from the kitchen, where ingredients are cooked with the help of hot vapor. It involves placing food above boiling water, allowing the steam to gently cook the ingredients.

- **Nutrient Retention:** Steaming is a gentle cooking method that helps retain the nutrients in vegetables, fish, and other delicate ingredients.

- **Tender and Moist:** Steaming keeps the food moist, preventing it from drying out and maintaining its natural flavors.

2. Boiling: Boiling is like a bubbly cauldron of flavors, where ingredients are immersed in boiling water and cooked until tender.

- **Quick and Efficient:** Boiling is a fast and efficient method, perfect for cooking pasta, rice, and vegetables in a short amount of time.
- **Al Dente Control:** Boiling allows you to achieve the desired texture, whether it's tender and fully cooked or slightly firm, known as "al dente."

Tips for Steaming and Boiling:

- **Use a Steamer Basket:** A steamer basket helps keep ingredients above the water level, allowing them to cook evenly.
- **Steaming Times:** Adjust steaming times based on the size and thickness of the ingredients to avoid overcooking.

- Salt the Water: When boiling, add a pinch of salt to enhance the flavors of the ingredients.
- Preserve Colors: When boiling vegetables, immerse them in ice-cold water after cooking to preserve their vibrant colors.

Steaming and boiling are the gentle caretakers of nutrients and textures, ensuring your dishes are both healthy and delicious. Embrace the moist and loving environment of these cooking techniques, and your ingredients will thank you with their tender and flavorful results.

Timing and Temperature: When to Apply Heat

Timing and temperature are like the conductors of a cooking symphony, ensuring that each ingredient performs at its best. Let's explore the importance of timing and temperature in applying heat to your dishes:

1. Timing Matters: Knowing when to apply heat is crucial in achieving the perfect results. Different ingredients and cooking techniques require varying amounts of time to reach their full potential.

- **Preheating:** Preheating your oven or pan ensures that the cooking process starts at the right temperature, promoting even and consistent cooking.
- **Cooking Time:** Pay attention to cooking times in recipes, as overcooking or undercooking can affect the texture and taste of your dishes.

2. Temperature Control: The right temperature is like the secret ingredient that unlocks the flavors in your ingredients. Different heat levels produce different results.

- **Low Heat:** Low heat is gentle and perfect for slow-cooking, simmering, and delicate ingredients that need time to develop flavors.
- **Medium Heat:** Medium heat is the go-to for sautéing, stir-frying, and achieving golden-brown crusts without burning.
- **High Heat:** High heat is intense and excellent for quick cooking, searing, and creating that delicious caramelization on meats and vegetables.

Tips for Timing and Temperature:

- **Use a Timer:** Set a timer to keep track of cooking times, avoiding overcooking or undercooking.
- **Adjust as Needed:** Be ready to adjust the temperature during cooking to maintain control and achieve the desired results.
- **Resting Time:** Allow your dishes to rest after cooking, giving them time to develop flavors and ensuring juiciness and tenderness.
- **Cooking with Confidence:** Practice and experience will help you become more confident in judging cooking times and temperatures.

Timing and temperature are the essential tools that ensure your culinary creations are a symphony of flavors and textures. Embrace the art of timing and temperature control, and your dishes will perform like culinary masterpieces that leave everyone applauding.

Preheating and Cooking Times

Preheating and cooking times are like the warm-up and main act of a cooking show, ensuring that your dishes shine with perfection. Let's dive into the importance of preheating and cooking times:

1. Preheating: Preheating your oven or pan is like giving it a head start, ensuring it reaches the right temperature before you start cooking.

- **Even Cooking:** Preheating helps your dish cook evenly from the beginning, avoiding any hot or cold spots that could affect the final result.
- **Baking Success:** For baking, preheating is essential to help your cakes, cookies, and breads rise and bake to perfection.

2. Cooking Times: Knowing how long to cook your dishes is like hitting the sweet spot for flavor and texture.

- **Follow Recipes:** Follow the cooking times mentioned in recipes as a guide, but also use your senses to judge doneness.
- **Test for Doneness:** Use a thermometer, fork, or knife to check if meats, vegetables, and baked goods are fully cooked.

Tips for Preheating and Cooking Times:

- Plan Ahead: Preheat your oven or pan while you're preparing ingredients to save time.
- Oven Thermometer: Consider using an oven thermometer to ensure your oven is accurate, especially for baking.
- Resting Time: Allow dishes to rest after cooking to allow flavors to meld and juices to redistribute.
- Practice Makes Perfect: As you cook more, you'll develop a sense of timing and know when dishes are cooked to perfection.

Preheating and cooking times are the dynamic duo that ensures your dishes steal the spotlight. Embrace the importance of giving your cooking a head start and cooking things for just the right amount of time, and your culinary performances will be show-stopping delights.

Resting and Carryover Cooking

Resting and carryover cooking are like the final touch of perfection for your dishes. Let's dive into these culinary secrets and how they work their magic:

1. Resting: Resting is like a little time-out for your food after cooking. Once your dish is done, you let it sit for a few minutes before serving.

- **Tender and Juicy:** Resting meats, like steaks or roasted poultry, allows the juices to redistribute, making them tender and juicy when you cut into them.
- **Flavors Unite:** During resting, the flavors in your dish mingle and harmonize, creating a more delicious and cohesive taste.

2. Carryover Cooking: Carryover cooking is like a surprise encore performance that happens after your food leaves the heat source.

- **Continued Heat:** Even after you remove your dish from direct heat, it keeps cooking for a short while due to the residual heat trapped inside.
- **Perfect Doneness:** Account for carryover cooking when gauging the doneness of your food to avoid overcooking.

Tips for Resting and Carryover Cooking:

- **Cover Lightly:** For meats, loosely cover them with foil during resting to keep them warm without trapping too much steam.
- **Be Patient:** Give larger cuts of meat a few minutes to rest, while baked goods may need a little time before slicing.
- **Check Temperature:** Use a food thermometer to monitor the internal temperature during resting to achieve the desired doneness.
- **Plan Ahead:** Factor in resting and carryover cooking when timing your meal to ensure everything is ready at the same time.

Resting and carryover cooking are the final touches that elevate your dishes to greatness. Embrace these simple yet powerful techniques, and your food will be a delicious triumph that impresses and satisfies every time.

Chapter 5

The Art of Combining Elements

Building Flavor Profiles: Understanding Combinations

Salt and Fat: Creating Richness and Depth

Building flavor profiles is like crafting a symphony of taste in your dishes, and two key players in this orchestra are salt and fat.

The Art of Combining Elements - Flavors unite in a culinary symphony, where salt, fat, acid, and heat play in perfect harmony."

1. Salt and Fat: These flavor superheroes work together to create richness and depth in your cooking.

• **Salt:** Think of salt as the conductor of flavor. It enhances the taste of ingredients, making them more vibrant and delicious. It balances sweetness, tones down bitterness, and boosts savory flavors. Just a pinch of salt can elevate your dish from ordinary to extraordinary!

- **Fat:** Fat is like the velvety background music that adds richness and mouthfeel to your food. Whether it's butter, oil, or animal fats, adding a touch of fat can make your dish feel more indulgent and satisfying.

Combining Salt and Fat: The magic happens when you combine salt and fat in your cooking. Salt enhances the natural flavors of your ingredients, and fat carries those flavors across your taste buds, making them linger and dance on your palate.

For example:

- Seasoning a steak with salt before grilling not only adds savory depth but also helps the meat retain moisture, making it juicier and more succulent.
- Drizzling olive oil and sprinkling salt on roasted vegetables not only enhances their natural sweetness but also gives them a luxurious, silky mouthfeel.

Remember, like any great symphony, balance is key! Use salt and fat in moderation to avoid overpowering the other flavors in your dish. And don't forget to taste as you go, adjusting the seasoning to create the perfect harmony.

Fat and Acid: Balancing Creaminess with Brightness

Building flavor profiles is like painting a masterpiece on your plate, and two essential brushstrokes are fat and acid.

1. **Fat:** Fat is like the velvety canvas that adds richness and creaminess to your dishes. It comes from sources like butter, oils, and animal fats. When you add fat to your cooking, it coats your taste buds, making everything feel more indulgent and satisfying.

2. **Acid:** Acid is like the vibrant splash of color that brings brightness and liveliness to your food. It comes from ingredients like citrus fruits, vinegar, and certain dairy products like yogurt. Acid cuts through the richness of fat, adding a tangy and refreshing touch to your dishes.

Combining Fat and Acid: The real magic happens when you combine fat and acid in your culinary artwork. They work together to strike a perfect balance

– the fat provides a luxurious, smooth base, while the acid brings a bright and zesty contrast.

For example:

- In a salad dressing, olive oil (fat) creates a silky texture, while balsamic vinegar (acid) adds a tangy kick that elevates the flavors of the greens and veggies.
- Creamy avocado (fat) paired with a squeeze of lime juice (acid) makes a delightful guacamole, with the richness of the avocado beautifully balanced by the zesty brightness of the lime.

Achieving the right balance between fat and acid is like finding the perfect harmony in your culinary creations. Just like a skilled artist, use these flavor elements thoughtfully to create a masterpiece on your taste buds.

Acid and Salt: Enhancing Flavors with a Pop of Tang

Building flavor profiles is like mixing colors on a palate, and two standout hues are acid and salt.

1. **Acid:** Acid is like the spark of brightness that wakes up your taste buds. It comes from ingredients like citrus fruits (lemons, limes), vinegar, and even certain dairy products (yogurt).

   When you add acid to your dish, it gives it a lively tang that makes everything taste more vibrant and refreshing.

2. **Salt:** Salt is like the anchor that grounds all the flavors together. It enhances the taste of your ingredients, making them more pronounced and balanced. Just a pinch of salt can transform an ordinary dish into something extraordinary.

Combining Acid and Salt: The real magic happens when you combine acid and salt in your culinary creations. They work together to elevate flavors with a delightful pop of tang and depth.

For example:

- A squeeze of lemon juice (acid) sprinkled with a pinch of salt over grilled fish not only adds a zesty kick but also enhances the natural sweetness of the seafood.

- A splash of vinegar (acid) and a sprinkle of salt in a tomato salad intensifies the tomato's taste and brightens up the whole dish.

Using acid and salt in harmony is like playing a perfect melody on your taste buds. Just like a skilled conductor, use these flavor elements thoughtfully to create a symphony of taste in your dishes.

Techniques for Harmonizing the Elements

Emulsification: Creating Creamy and Stable Mixtures

Harmonizing the elements in cooking is like orchestrating a beautiful melody of flavors, and one powerful technique for creating creamy and stable mixtures is emulsification.

Emulsification: Emulsification is like a culinary magic trick that brings together usually unmixable ingredients, like oil and water, into a smooth and creamy blend. It's all about creating a stable mixture by breaking up one liquid into tiny droplets and dispersing them throughout the other liquid.

How it works: Imagine a conductor leading an orchestra – in emulsification, an emulsifying agent (like egg yolk, mustard, or honey) acts as the maestro. It has molecules that are attracted to both water and oil. When you whisk or blend the emulsifying agent with the two liquids, it coats the tiny droplets of oil with a protective layer, preventing them from clumping together and separating from the water.

Mayonnaise: A superstar example of emulsification is mayonnaise. When you whisk egg yolk with oil and a splash of vinegar or lemon juice, the egg yolk acts as the emulsifying agent. It brings the oil and vinegar together into a creamy, stable sauce that's simply magical on sandwiches or salads.

Dressings and Sauces: Emulsification is essential for creating luscious dressings and sauces, like vinaigrettes or hollandaise sauce. By blending oil with vinegar or citrus juice while adding an emulsifying agent, you get a smooth and velvety mixture that clings deliciously to your greens or eggs Benedict.

Mastering emulsification is like adding a secret weapon to your cooking arsenal. So, the next time you want to create creamy and stable mixtures, think of emulsification as your culinary wand, and watch the flavors come together in perfect harmony!

Balancing and Adjusting Flavors throughout the Cooking Process

Balancing and adjusting flavors throughout the cooking process is the key to creating a delicious symphony on your plate!

1. Balancing Flavors: Imagine a tightrope walker finding the perfect balance – that's what you do with flavors. Different tastes like sweetness, saltiness, sourness, bitterness, and umami need to be in harmony. When one flavor is too dominant, the dish can taste off-balance.

- **Sweetness:** It adds a pleasant, sugary note to your dish, but be careful not to make it too cloying.
- **Saltiness:** It enhances flavors, but too much can overpower other tastes.
- **Sourness:** It brings brightness and tanginess, but excessive sourness can be overwhelming.

- **Bitterness:** In moderation, it can add depth, but too much can make the dish unpalatable.
- **Umami:** It's the savory, mouthwatering taste that complements other flavors.

2. Adjusting Flavors: Like a skilled DJ, you can fine-tune the flavors throughout cooking to achieve a perfect mix.

- **Taste as you go:** Continuously sample your dish during cooking. This helps you detect any imbalances and adjust accordingly.
- **Add gradually:** When adding seasonings or flavor enhancers, do it slowly and in small increments. You can always add more, but you can't take it back once it's in there!
- **Counterbalance:** If a flavor is too strong, balance it out with a complementary taste. For example, if a dish is too salty, a splash of lemon juice can help cut through the saltiness.
- **Texture matters:** Remember that texture plays a role in flavor perception. The right crunch or creaminess can elevate the overall experience.

By actively balancing and adjusting flavors throughout the cooking process, you become the master chef of taste. Your dishes will sing with a perfect blend of flavors, leaving everyone's taste buds applauding! Happy cooking!

Pairing Elements with Different Cuisines and Dishes

Pairing elements with different cuisines and dishes is the secret to crafting unique and delicious flavors!

1. Flavor Pairing: Just like best friends who bring out the best in each other, some ingredients have natural affinities. By pairing complementary flavors, you can enhance the overall taste of your dish.

- **Sweet and Savory:** In many cuisines, combining sweetness with savory elements creates a balanced and intriguing profile. Think of honey-glazed chicken or teriyaki sauce.
- **Spicy and Cooling:** In spicy dishes, cooling ingredients like yogurt or cucumber raita can tame the heat and provide a refreshing contrast.

- **Acid and Fat:** Tangy ingredients like lemon juice or vinegar can cut through the richness of fatty dishes, adding brightness and balance.

2. Cuisines and Dishes: Like traveling the world through food, different cuisines offer unique combinations of flavors. Understanding the key elements in each cuisine helps you pair ingredients that complement their traditional dishes.

- **Italian Cuisine:** Embrace the simplicity of Italian flavors with the holy trinity of tomatoes, garlic, and basil. Add some olive oil and cheese, and you're on the path to a classic Italian dish.
- **Asian Cuisine:** Explore the complexity of Asian flavors with soy sauce, ginger, and garlic. Combine the umami of soy sauce with the heat of chili peppers for a tantalizing stir-fry.
- **Indian Cuisine:** Dive into the rich and aromatic world of Indian spices like cumin, coriander, and turmeric. Embrace the creaminess of yogurt in curries and pair it with the heat of chili for a delightful balance.

By playing the role of a flavor matchmaker, you can create a symphony of taste in your cooking. Experiment with different ingredients and cuisines, and let your creativity lead the way to mouthwatering culinary experiences! Happy cooking and happy pairing!

Chapter 6

Beyond the Basics

Exploring Additional Cooking Techniques

Caramelization: Unlocking Sweetness and Complexity

Exploring additional cooking techniques is like embarking on a flavorful adventure, and one exciting technique to discover is caramelization!

Caramelization: Caramelization is like a sweet transformation that unlocks the hidden sweetness and complexity of certain ingredients. It happens when sugars in food undergo a magical reaction when exposed to heat.

"Unleashing culinary artistry, soaring to new flavors, and reaching extraordinary heights."

How it works: When you apply heat to ingredients containing natural sugars, like onions, carrots, or even sugar itself, something extraordinary happens. The sugars start to break down and turn into a rich, golden-brown caramel. This process adds depth and complexity to the flavors, creating a delightful balance of sweet and savory notes.

Key Ingredients: Some ingredients are more prone to caramelization than others. Onions, for instance, undergo a magical metamorphosis when slowly cooked, turning into sweet, caramelized strands that add a wonderful dimension to many dishes.

Uses in Cooking: Caramelization is like a secret weapon in the kitchen, elevating both savory and sweet dishes.

- In savory dishes, caramelized onions can add a delightful sweetness to soups, stews, and even burgers.
- In desserts, caramelized sugar creates the luscious caramel sauce that makes everything irresistible.

Tips: To achieve the perfect caramelization, remember to:

- **Use moderate heat:** Caramelization takes time, so be patient and avoid high heat that may burn the sugars.
- **Stir occasionally:** Give the sugars a gentle nudge to prevent uneven browning.
- **Add a touch of water:** For certain ingredients, adding a splash of water can help kickstart the caramelization process.

Maillard Reaction: Browning and Flavor Development

Maillard Reaction: The Maillard reaction is like a flavor fireworks show that happens when proteins and sugars dance together under heat. It's a magical browning process that creates delicious depths of flavor and enticing aromas in your food.

How it works: When you cook certain foods, like meat, bread, or even cookies, the natural sugars and proteins present start to tango when exposed to heat. As they dance, they create a complex network of new flavor compounds, resulting in the mouthwatering browning effect we all love.

Browning and Flavor: The Maillard reaction is like the artist's brushstroke that adds richness and depth to your dishes. It gives your steaks a tantalizing crust, your bread a golden hue, and your chocolate chip cookies that irresistible aroma.

Versatility: The Maillard reaction is not picky; it can happen in a variety of cooking methods.

- Pan-searing a steak creates the sought-after caramelized crust.
- Baking bread turns the dough into a beautiful golden loaf.
- Roasting vegetables intensifies their flavors and gives them a lovely browned edge.

Tips: To get the most out of the Maillard reaction, remember to:

- **Dry the surface:** Moisture on the surface of the food can slow down browning, so pat dry before cooking.
- **Don't overcrowd:** Leave space between ingredients to ensure even browning and prevent steaming.

- **Pay attention:** Browning can happen quickly, so keep an eye on your food to avoid burning.

Confit: Preservation and Tenderization

Confit: Confit is like a culinary time capsule that combines preservation and tenderization in a mouthwatering way. It's a traditional French technique used to slow-cook meat, usually duck, chicken, or pork, in its own fat or oil, along with aromatic herbs and spices.

How it works: When you confit something, you gently cook it at a low temperature in a flavorful fat bath, which could be duck fat, olive oil, or any other oil of your choice. The fat acts as a magical protector, sealing in the meat's natural juices while cooking it slowly and evenly.

Preservation and Tenderization: Confit is like a preservation wizard that keeps your food tender and flavorful for an extended period. The slow-cooking process breaks down tough fibers in the meat, making it incredibly tender. Additionally, the fat acts as a seal, preserving the meat and extending its shelf life.

Versatility: While the classic confit involves meat, you can apply this technique to various ingredients.

- Garlic cloves can be confit in olive oil, becoming soft, mellow, and perfect for spreads.
- Fruits like tomatoes or even lemons can be confit for a concentrated burst of flavor.

Uses: The tender and flavorful results of confit make it a versatile technique in the kitchen.

- Serve duck confit with crispy skin and tender meat, paired with greens or potatoes.
- Use garlic confit as a spread or blend it into sauces for a subtle, nutty flavor.
- Confit lemons add depth and complexity to dressings and marinades.

Tips: To achieve the best results when confiting, remember to:

- Use enough fat to fully submerge the ingredient for even cooking and preservation.
- Cook at a low temperature, maintaining a gentle simmer, and avoid rapid boiling.

- Store the confit in its cooking fat for optimal preservation.

Developing Your Palate: Tasting and Adjusting

Identifying Flavor Imbalances and Solutions

Developing your palate is like becoming a taste detective – training your taste buds to detect flavors and creating perfectly balanced dishes. Here's how you can become a flavor expert by tasting and adjusting:

1. Tasting and Adjusting: Think of tasting as your superpower in the kitchen. As you cook, take time to sample your dishes at different stages. This helps you understand the flavors and identify any imbalances.

- **Use all your senses:** Smell the aromas, observe the colors, and feel the textures. Engaging all your senses enhances your tasting experience.
- **Take notes:** Keep a flavor journal to jot down your observations and adjustments. It will help you remember what works and what needs improvement.

2. Identifying Flavor Imbalances: Becoming a flavor detective means spotting when something doesn't taste quite right. Common imbalances include:

- **Too salty:** If your dish is too salty, balance it with a touch of sweetness (sugar, honey) or acidity (lemon juice, vinegar).
- **Too bland:** Lack of flavor calls for more seasoning. Add a pinch of salt, spices, or herbs to wake up the taste.
- **Too bitter:** Combat bitterness with a bit of sweetness or creaminess. Honey or a splash of cream can do wonders.
- **Too sour:** Counter sourness with a touch of sweetness or even a pinch of salt.

3. Solutions: Like a culinary problem-solver, you have a range of ingredients to balance flavors:

- **Sweetness:** Sugar, honey, maple syrup.
- **Saltiness:** Salt, soy sauce, miso paste.
- **Acidity:** Lemon juice, vinegar, yogurt.
- **Umami:** Soy sauce, mushrooms, tomatoes.

Remember, finding the perfect balance takes practice. Trust your taste buds and don't be afraid to experiment with adjustments. Over time, you'll develop a refined palate that creates amazing dishes!

So, put on your detective hat, and embark on a flavorful journey. Tasting and adjusting will transform your cooking, making you the master of perfectly balanced flavors.

Experimenting with Seasonings and Flavors

Here's how to unlock your taste potential by tasting, adjusting, and fearlessly experimenting with seasonings and flavors:

1. Experimenting with Seasonings and Flavors: Be a fearless flavor pioneer! Don't be afraid to try new seasonings and combinations to add excitement to your dishes.

- Start with familiar ingredients: Begin with spices and herbs you know and love, then gradually introduce new ones.
- **Pair wisely:** Experiment with flavors that complement each other. Sweet and spicy, tangy and savory – mix and match to find surprising harmonies.

- **Take small steps:** When trying a new seasoning, start with a little and build up gradually. You can always add more, but you can't take it away!

2. Embrace Umami: Don't forget the fifth taste sensation – umami! Umami-rich ingredients like soy sauce, mushrooms, and tomatoes can elevate your dishes to new heights.

3. Be Curious and Creative: Cooking is an art, and you're the artist. Let your curiosity guide you and don't be afraid to be creative. Try new combinations and trust your instincts.

Remember, developing your palate is a journey of discovery. Every taste and adjustment brings you closer to becoming a flavor virtuoso. So, put on your apron and embark on this exciting flavor expedition. Happy tasting, adjusting, and experimenting! Your taste buds will thank you for the delicious adventure!

Applying the Four Elements to Baking and Desserts

Incorporating Salt, Fat, Acid, and Heat in Baked Goods

Applying the four elements of salt, fat, acid, and heat to baking and desserts is like creating a symphony of flavors and textures in your sweet treats. Let's explore how these elements play a magical role in making your baked goods extraordinary:

1. Salt: Salt in baking may seem counterintuitive, but it's the conductor that brings out the best in flavors. Just a pinch enhances sweetness, balances bitterness, and creates a harmonious taste in your treats.

- In cookies and cakes, a small amount of salt can elevate the overall flavor profile, making it more enjoyable.

2. Fat: Fat in baking is like the artist's brush that adds richness and tenderness to your creations.

Butter, oil, or shortening are commonly used to make baked goods moist and delectable.

- In cookies, fat contributes to a soft, chewy texture, while in pie crusts, it creates flakiness and richness.

3. Acid: Acid in baking is like the bright star that adds zing and balance to the sweetness. It can come from ingredients like citrus juices, vinegar, or yogurt.

- In muffins and cakes, a touch of lemon zest or buttermilk can create a delightful tangy contrast to the sweetness.

4. Heat: Heat is like the wizard's spell that transforms raw ingredients into golden wonders. The right temperature and baking time are essential to achieve perfect textures and flavors.

- In cakes and bread, the right baking temperature ensures a tender crumb and a golden crust.

By incorporating the four elements into your baking, you're like a flavor magician, conjuring delightful desserts that leave everyone craving for more. So, the next time you bake, don't forget the magic of salt, fat, acid, and heat to create enchanting and irresistible treats! Happy baking!

Balancing Flavors in Desserts and Sweet Treats

Applying the four elements of flavor to desserts is like crafting a delicious masterpiece that makes taste buds dance with joy. Let's dive into how these elements work together to balance flavors in sweet treats:

1. Salt: Salt in desserts may seem surprising, but it's the secret ingredient that enhances and balances other flavors. It adds depth and makes the sweetness pop.

- In chocolate desserts, a pinch of salt elevates the richness and intensifies the chocolate flavor.

2. Fat: Fat in desserts is like the velvety blanket that provides richness and indulgence. It adds a luxurious mouthfeel and keeps desserts moist.

- In creamy desserts like cheesecakes or mousses, the fat from cream cheese or whipped cream gives a smooth and luscious texture.

3. Acid: Acid in desserts is like the bright spark that cuts through sweetness, preventing it from becoming cloying. It adds a refreshing and zesty element.

- In fruit-based desserts, a splash of lemon juice or a hint of citrus zest balances the sweetness and adds a delightful tang.

4. Heat: Heat in desserts is the magical oven that transforms raw ingredients into mouthwatering delights. The right baking or cooking temperature is essential for perfect textures and flavors.

- In baked goods like pies and cookies, the right amount of heat ensures even baking, creating golden crusts and tender centers.

Balancing Flavors: Like a flavor conductor, balancing these elements is crucial to creating delightful desserts.

- **Taste as you go:** While preparing your desserts, taste the mixture at different stages. Adjust the sweetness, acidity, or saltiness to find the perfect balance.

- **Contrast and complement:** Pair flavors that contrast and complement each other. Sweet with tangy, creamy with crunchy – these combinations create exciting flavor experiences.

- **Keep it simple:** Sometimes, less is more. Focus on a few key flavors to let them shine.

By applying the four elements and balancing flavors in your desserts, you'll create delightful treats that leave a lasting impression. So, let your creativity and taste buds guide you on this sweet adventure.

Note

Part II

Chapter 7

Recipes and Essential Kitchen Tools Recommendations

Kitchen Tools Recommendations

For the "Salt, Fat, Acid, Heat Cookbook for Beginners," we recommend a selection of essential kitchen tools that will help beginners confidently navigate the recipes and techniques presented in the cookbook. These tools are versatile, user-friendly, and essential for achieving delicious results. Let's dive into the recommendations:

1. Measuring Tools:

- **Kitchen Scale:** For precise measurements of ingredients, especially for baking and cooking.
- **Measuring Cups and Spoons:** To accurately measure liquids, dry ingredients, and spices.

2. Cutting and Chopping:

- Chef's Knife: A versatile and sharp knife for slicing, dicing, and chopping.
- Cutting Board: A durable and spacious surface to safely prepare ingredients.

3. Cooking and Baking:

- **Skillet:** A versatile pan for sautéing, frying, and searing.
- **Saucepan:** Perfect for simmering, boiling, and preparing sauces.

"Inspire your inner chef with our mouthwatering recipes, and discover the must-have kitchen tools that will make cooking a delightful and effortless art."

- **Baking Sheet:** For baking cookies, roasting vegetables, and more.
- **Mixing Bowls:** A set of bowls in various sizes for mixing ingredients.

4. Food Preparation:

- **Grater:** For shredding cheese, vegetables, and zesting citrus fruits.
- **Garlic Press:** An efficient tool for crushing garlic cloves.
- **Citrus Juicer:** For easily extracting juice from lemons, limes, and oranges.

5. Baking Essentials:

- Rolling Pin: A must-have for rolling out dough for pies, cookies, and pastries.
- Pastry Brush: To apply egg washes, melted butter, and glazes.
- Whisk: Ideal for beating eggs, mixing batters, and creating smooth sauces.

6. Presentation and Serving:

- **Tongs:** For flipping and turning food while cooking.
- **Serving Platters:** Elegant platters to present and showcase your culinary creations.
- **Salad Spinner:** For washing and drying salad greens efficiently.

7. Food Safety and Cleanliness:

- **Food Thermometer:** To ensure meats and dishes are cooked to the correct temperature.
- **Oven Mitts:** For safely handling hot pots, pans, and baking dishes.
- **Kitchen Timer:** To keep track of cooking and resting times.

These essential kitchen tools will make your cooking experience more enjoyable and productive. Whether you're a beginner or an experienced home cook, having these tools at your disposal will empower you to master the art of salt, fat, acid, and heat in your culinary creations.

Recipes Recommendations

Appetizers and Starters

Recipe 1: Creamy Avocado Dip (Fat and Acid)

Ingredients:

- 2 ripe avocados
- 1 lime, juiced
- 1 clove garlic, minced
- 1/4 cup plain Greek yogurt
- 2 tablespoons chopped fresh cilantro
- Salt and pepper to taste

Instructions:

1. Cut the avocados in half, remove the pits, and scoop the flesh into a mixing bowl.

2. Add the lime juice and minced garlic to the avocados.

3. Mash the avocado mixture with a fork until smooth, leaving some chunks for texture.

4. Stir in the Greek yogurt and chopped cilantro.

5. Season the dip with salt and pepper to taste, adjusting the seasonings as needed.

6. Transfer the creamy avocado dip to a serving bowl and garnish with extra cilantro if desired.

Prep and Cooking Time: 10 minutes

Serving Size: Makes about 1 1/2 cups of dip

Nutritional Information (per serving - 2 tablespoons):

- Calories: 50
- Fat: 4g
- Carbohydrates: 3g
- Protein: 1g
- Fiber: 2g

Ingredients Substitutions:

- If Greek yogurt is not available, you can use sour cream or mayonnaise for a creamier texture.
- For added heat, add a finely chopped jalapeño or a pinch of red pepper flakes.

Tips and Tricks:

- To prevent browning, place the avocado pits back into the dip or cover the surface with plastic wrap before refrigerating.
- For an extra tangy flavor, you can add a splash of hot sauce or a sprinkle of cumin.

Recipe 2: Caprese Salad (Salt and Acid)

Ingredients:

- 2 large ripe tomatoes, sliced
- 8 oz fresh mozzarella, sliced
- Fresh basil leaves
- 2 tablespoons balsamic vinegar
- 2 tablespoons extra-virgin olive oil
- Salt and pepper to taste

Instructions:

1. Arrange the tomato slices and mozzarella slices alternately on a serving platter.
2. Tuck fresh basil leaves between the tomato and mozzarella slices.
3. Drizzle the balsamic vinegar and olive oil over the salad.
4. Season with salt and pepper to taste.
5. Serve the Caprese salad immediately as a refreshing appetizer or side dish.

Prep and Cooking Time: 15 minutes

Serving Size: Serves 4

Nutritional Information (per serving):

- Calories: 180
- Fat: 14g
- Carbohydrates: 4g
- Protein: 10g
- Fiber: 1g

Ingredients Substitutions:

- Replace balsamic vinegar with red wine vinegar for a slightly different tang.

- Use cherry tomatoes and mini mozzarella balls for a fun twist on traditional Caprese salad.

Tips and Tricks:

- For a beautiful presentation, stack the tomato, mozzarella, and basil leaves vertically to create a tower.
- If you have fresh heirloom tomatoes, they will add even more vibrant colors and flavors to the salad.

Main Courses

Recipe 3: Lemon-Herb Roast Chicken (Salt, Fat, Acid, and Heat)

Ingredients:

- 1 whole chicken (about 4-5 pounds)
- 2 lemons, zested and juiced
- 4 cloves garlic, minced
- 2 tablespoons fresh thyme, chopped
- 2 tablespoons fresh rosemary, chopped
- 1/4 cup olive oil
- Kosher Salt and black pepper to taste

Instructions:

1. Preheat the oven to 425°F (220°C).

2. In a small bowl, mix the lemon zest, lemon juice, minced garlic, chopped thyme, rosemary, and olive oil to make the marinade.

3. Pat the chicken dry with paper towels and season it generously with salt and pepper, both inside and out.

4. Rub the lemon-herb marinade all over the chicken, making sure to get under the skin and inside the cavity.

5. Place the chicken on a roasting pan or a baking dish, breast side up.

6. Roast the chicken in the preheated oven for about 1 hour and 15 minutes or until the internal temperature reaches 165°F (74°C) in the thickest part of the thigh.

7. Let the chicken rest for 10 minutes before carving and serving.

Prep and Cooking Time: 1 hour and 30 minutes

Serving Size: Serves 4-6

Nutritional Information (per serving):

- Calories: 350
- Fat: 22g
- Carbohydrates: 2g
- Protein: 34g
- Fiber: 1g

Ingredients Substitutions:

- If you prefer a different herb combination, you can use parsley, sage, or oregano instead of thyme and rosemary.
- Replace olive oil with melted butter for a richer flavor.

Tips and Tricks:

- To ensure even cooking, truss the chicken by tying the legs together with kitchen twine.
- For crispy skin, you can broil the chicken for the last 5 minutes, keeping an eye on it to avoid burning.

Recipe 4: Garlic Butter Shrimp Pasta (Fat and Salt)

Ingredients:

- 8 oz linguine or spaghetti
- 1 pound large shrimp, peeled and deveined
- 4 tablespoons unsalted butter
- 4 cloves garlic, minced
- 1/4 teaspoon red pepper flakes (optional, for heat)
- 1/4 cup chopped fresh parsley
- Salt and pepper to taste
- Grated Parmesan cheese for serving

Instructions:

1. Cook the pasta according to the package instructions until al dente. Drain and set aside.

2. In a large skillet, melt the butter over medium heat. Add the minced garlic and red pepper flakes (if using) and sauté for about 1 minute until fragrant.

3. Add the shrimp to the skillet and cook for 2-3 minutes on each side until they turn pink and opaque. Season with salt and pepper.

4. Toss the cooked pasta with the garlic butter shrimp in the skillet until well combined.

5. Sprinkle chopped parsley over the pasta and toss again.

6. Serve the garlic butter shrimp pasta hot, garnished with grated Parmesan cheese if desired.

Prep and Cooking Time: 20 minutes

Serving Size: Serves 4

Nutritional Information (per serving):

- Calories: 420
- Fat: 15g
- Carbohydrates: 46g
- Protein: 28g
- Fiber: 2g

Ingredients Substitutions:

- Replace linguine or spaghetti with your favorite pasta shape.
- Use ghee or olive oil instead of butter for a dairy-free version.

Tips and Tricks:

- For added richness, drizzle a bit of extra-virgin olive oil over the pasta just before serving.
- Enhance the flavors with a squeeze of lemon juice or a splash of white wine during the shrimp cooking process.

Sides and Vegetables

Recipe 5: Roasted Brussels Sprouts with Balsamic Glaze (Salt and Acid)

Ingredients:

- 1 pound Brussels sprouts, trimmed and halved
- 2 tablespoons olive oil
- Kosher Salt and pepper to taste
- 2 tablespoons balsamic vinegar
- 1 tablespoon honey (optional, for sweetness)
- 2 tablespoons grated Parmesan cheese (optional, for garnish)

Instructions:

1. Preheat the oven to 400°F (200°C).

2. In a large mixing bowl, toss the halved Brussels sprouts with olive oil, salt, and pepper until well coated.

3. Spread the Brussels sprouts in a single layer on a baking sheet.

4. Roast the Brussels sprouts in the preheated oven for 20-25 minutes or until they are tender and slightly caramelized.

5. In a small saucepan, combine the balsamic vinegar and honey (if using). Bring to a simmer over medium heat and cook for 1-2 minutes until the glaze slightly thickens.

6. Drizzle the balsamic glaze over the roasted Brussels sprouts and toss to coat evenly.

7. Garnish with grated Parmesan cheese (if desired) and serve immediately.

Prep and Cooking Time: 30 minutes

Serving Size: Serves 4

Nutritional Information (per serving):

- Calories: 120
- Fat: 7g
- Carbohydrates: 14g

- Protein: 4g
- Fiber: 4g

Ingredients Substitutions:

- Use any other vegetables you enjoy roasting, such as cauliflower or carrots.
- Maple syrup or brown sugar can be substituted for honey to add sweetness to the glaze.

Tips and Tricks:

- For a nutty crunch, add some toasted pine nuts or sliced almonds to the roasted Brussels sprouts before serving.
- Balsamic glaze can be found in stores, or you can make your own by reducing balsamic vinegar on low heat until it thickens.

Recipe 6: Creamy Mashed Potatoes (Fat and Salt)

Ingredients:

- 2 pounds russet potatoes, peeled and cut into chunks
- 1/2 cup whole milk or heavy cream
- 4 tablespoons unsalted butter
- Salt and pepper to taste
- Fresh chives or parsley, chopped (optional, for garnish)

Instructions:

1. In a large pot, add the potato chunks and cover with cold water. Bring to a boil over high heat and cook until the potatoes are fork-tender, about 15-20 minutes.
2. Drain the potatoes and return them to the pot.
3. Add the milk or heavy cream and butter to the potatoes.
4. Mash the potatoes with a potato masher or use a hand mixer for a smoother consistency.
5. Season the mashed potatoes with salt and pepper to taste, adjusting as needed.
6. Transfer the creamy mashed potatoes to a serving bowl and garnish with chopped chives or parsley (if desired).

Prep and Cooking Time: 25 minutes

Serving Size: Serves 4-6

Nutritional Information (per serving):

- Calories: 280
- Fat: 11g
- Carbohydrates: 41g

- Protein: 5g
- Fiber: 4g

Ingredients Substitutions:

- Use Yukon Gold potatoes for a creamier texture or red potatoes for a chunkier mash.
- Replace whole milk or heavy cream with unsweetened almond milk for a dairy-free alternative.

Tips and Tricks:

- For an extra luxurious touch, add a splash of truffle oil or a dollop of sour cream to the mashed potatoes.
- Be careful not to over-mix the potatoes, as this can make them gummy. Stop mashing as soon as they reach your desired consistency.

Desserts and Sweets

Recipe 7: Chocolate Salted Caramel Brownies (Salt, Fat, and Sweet)

Ingredients:

- 1 cup (2 sticks) unsalted butter
- 2 cups granulated sugar
- 4 large eggs
- 1 teaspoon vanilla extract
- 1 cup all-purpose flour
- 3/4 cup unsweetened cocoa powder
- 1/2 teaspoon salt
- 1/2 cup salted caramel sauce (store-bought or homemade)
- Sea salt flakes for sprinkling

Instructions:

1. Preheat the oven to 350°F (175°C). Grease and line a 9x9-inch baking pan with parchment paper, leaving an overhang on two sides for easy removal.
2. In a microwave-safe bowl, melt the butter. Stir in the granulated sugar until well combined.
3. Beat in the eggs one at a time, then add the vanilla extract and mix until smooth.
4. In a separate bowl, whisk together the flour, cocoa powder, and salt.

5. Gradually add the dry ingredients to the wet ingredients, stirring until just combined.

6. Pour half of the brownie batter into the prepared baking pan. Drizzle the salted caramel sauce over the batter, then top with the remaining batter.

7. Use a knife or toothpick to swirl the batter and caramel sauce together gently.

8. Bake the brownies in the preheated oven for 25-30 minutes or until a toothpick inserted into the center comes out with a few moist crumbs.

9. Remove the brownies from the oven and sprinkle with sea salt flakes while they are still warm.

10. Allow the brownies to cool completely in the pan before lifting them out using the parchment paper overhang.

11. Cut into squares and serve. Enjoy the gooey, chocolatey, and sweet-salty goodness!

Prep and Cooking Time: 45 minutes

Serving Size: Makes about 16 brownies

Nutritional Information (per brownie):

- Calories: 250
- Fat: 14g
- Carbohydrates: 32g
- Protein: 3g
- Fiber: 1g

Ingredients Substitutions:

- For a richer flavor, use dark chocolate cocoa powder instead of regular cocoa powder.
- If salted caramel sauce is not available, you can use regular caramel sauce and add a pinch of sea salt.

Tips and Tricks:

- For an extra decadent treat, top the cooled brownies with a scoop of vanilla ice cream and extra salted caramel sauce.
- Store any leftover brownies in an airtight container at room temperature for up to 3 days.

Recipe 8: Lemon Ricotta Cake (Fat and Acid)

Ingredients:

- 1 cup (2 sticks) unsalted butter, softened
- 1 1/2 cups granulated sugar
- 4 large eggs
- 1 teaspoon vanilla extract
- 1 1/2 cups all-purpose flour
- 1/2 cup almond flour
- 2 teaspoons baking powder
- 1/2 teaspoon salt
- 1 cup ricotta cheese
- Zest of 2 lemons
- Juice of 1 lemon
- Powdered sugar for dusting

Instructions:

1. Preheat the oven to 350°F (175°C). Grease and flour a 9-inch round cake pan.
2. In a large mixing bowl, cream together the softened butter and granulated sugar until light and fluffy.
3. Beat in the eggs one at a time, then add the vanilla extract and mix until well combined.

4. In a separate bowl, whisk together the all-purpose flour, almond flour, baking powder, and salt.
5. Gradually add the dry ingredients to the wet ingredients, alternating with the ricotta cheese.
6. Stir in the lemon zest and lemon juice, mixing until the batter is smooth and well incorporated.
7. Pour the batter into the prepared cake pan and spread it evenly.
8. Bake the cake in the preheated oven for 40-45 minutes or until a toothpick inserted into the center comes out clean.
9. Remove the cake from the oven and let it cool in the pan for 10 minutes before transferring it to a wire rack to cool completely.
10. Dust the lemon ricotta cake with powdered sugar before serving.

Prep and Cooking Time: 1 hour and 15 minutes

Serving Size: Serves 10-12

Nutritional Information (per serving):

- Calories: 360

- Fat: 20g
- Carbohydrates: 39g
- Protein: 6g
- Fiber: 1g

Ingredients Substitutions:

- If almond flour is not available, you can use all-purpose flour instead.
- Replace ricotta cheese with Greek yogurt for a tangy twist.

Tips and Tricks:

- For a more intense lemon flavor, drizzle the cooled cake with a lemon glaze made from lemon juice and powdered sugar.
- Serve the lemon ricotta cake with a dollop of whipped cream or a side of fresh berries for a delightful dessert.

Beverages and Cocktails

Recipe 9: Classic Margarita (Salt and Acid)

Ingredients:

- 2 oz tequila
- 1 oz triple sec or orange liqueur
- 1 oz freshly squeezed lime juice
- 1/2 oz simple syrup (optional, adjust to taste)
- Ice cubes
- Lime wedges and salt for garnish

Instructions:

1. Run a lime wedge along the rim of a glass to moisten it, then dip the rim in salt to coat.
2. Fill the glass with ice cubes.
3. In a cocktail shaker, combine the tequila, triple sec, lime juice, and simple syrup (if using).
4. Shake the mixture well to combine and chill the drink.
5. Strain the margarita into the prepared glass over ice.
6. Garnish with a lime wedge and serve immediately.

Prep and Cooking Time: 5 minutes

Serving Size: Makes 1 cocktail

Nutritional Information (per serving):

- Calories: 200
- Carbohydrates: 15g
- Protein: 0g
- Fat: 0g
- Fiber: 0g
- Ingredients Substitutions:
- Use mezcal instead of tequila for a smokier flavor.
- Replace triple sec with Cointreau or Grand Marnier for a premium margarita.

Tips and Tricks:

- For a frozen margarita, blend all the ingredients with ice until smooth.
- Adjust the sweetness of the margarita by adding more or less simple syrup to suit your taste preference.

Recipe 10: Avocado Banana Smoothie (Fat and Sweet)

Ingredients:

- 1 ripe avocado, peeled and pitted
- 1 ripe banana
- 1 cup milk (regular or plant-based)
- 1 tablespoon honey or maple syrup
- 1/2 teaspoon vanilla extract
- Ice cubes

Instructions:

1. In a blender, combine the peeled avocado, banana, milk, honey (or maple syrup), and vanilla extract.
2. Blend the ingredients until smooth and creamy.
3. Add ice cubes to the blender and blend again until the smoothie reaches your desired consistency.
4. Pour the avocado banana smoothie into a glass and serve immediately.

Prep and Cooking Time: 5 minutes

Serving Size: Makes 1 smoothie

Nutritional Information (per serving):

- Calories: 380
- Carbohydrates: 51g
- Protein: 6g
- Fat: 18g
- Fiber: 11g

Ingredients Substitutions:

- Use almond milk, soy milk, or coconut milk for a dairy-free option.
- Replace honey or maple syrup with agave syrup for a vegan alternative.

Tips and Tricks:

- For added creaminess, you can use frozen banana chunks instead of fresh banana.
- Customize the smoothie by adding a handful of spinach or kale for added nutrients.

Note

Conclusion

In conclusion, "The Salt, Fat, Acid, Heat Cookbook for Beginners" is a delightful culinary journey that empowers aspiring cooks to master the fundamental elements of flavor. From understanding the art of seasoning with salt to harnessing the richness of fats, from embracing the brightness of acids to applying the magic of heat, this cookbook serves as a trusted guide for creating delicious dishes that truly sing.

By demystifying the essential cooking techniques and providing clear, concise, and engaging explanations, this cookbook equips beginners with the confidence to explore their palates, experiment fearlessly, and achieve perfect balance in every dish. Through the exploration of various cuisines and techniques, the book encourages the development of a diverse and versatile cooking repertoire.

With each turn of the page, readers embark on a flavorful adventure, discovering the immense power that lies within the simple elements of salt, fat, acid, and heat. From savory to sweet, from stovetop to oven, this cookbook unlocks the secrets to transforming basic ingredients into culinary masterpieces.

So, whether you're a novice in the kitchen or a seasoned home cook looking to refine your skills, the "Salt, Fat, Acid, Heat Cookbook for Beginners" is the ideal companion on your culinary journey. With its emphasis on simplicity, clarity, and delectable results, it invites cooks of all levels to savor the joy of creating unforgettable meals that celebrate the beauty of taste and balance. Happy cooking!

Appendix

Measurement Conversions

Measurement conversions for the four elements (salt, fat, acid, and heat) are like the secret codes that unlock culinary versatility. Let's demystify these conversions and make them easy to understand:

1. Salt:

- 1 teaspoon of salt = approximately 5 grams
- 1 tablespoon of salt = approximately 15 grams

2. Fat (Oil, Butter, etc.):

- 1 teaspoon of oil or butter = approximately 5 grams

- 1 tablespoon of oil or butter = approximately 15 grams
- 1 cup of oil or butter = approximately 240 grams

3. Acid (Vinegar, Lemon Juice, etc.):

- 1 teaspoon of vinegar or lemon juice = approximately 5 milliliters
- 1 tablespoon of vinegar or lemon juice = approximately 15 milliliters
- 1 cup of vinegar or lemon juice = approximately 240 milliliters

4. Heat (Oven Temperature):

- 350°F (Fahrenheit) = approximately 175°C (Celsius)
- 400°F (Fahrenheit) = approximately 200°C (Celsius)
- 450°F (Fahrenheit) = approximately 230°C (Celsius)

Tips for Measurement Conversions:

- Use a Kitchen Scale: For accurate measurements, invest in a kitchen scale to weigh ingredients precisely.
- Online Conversion Tools: Online converters can be helpful in converting between different units quickly.
- Practice Makes Perfect: The more you cook and use these conversions, the more familiar and effortless they become.

Measurement conversions for the four elements are the keys to unlocking a world of cooking possibilities. Embrace these conversions, and you'll confidently navigate recipes from around the globe, creating delicious dishes with ease. Happy cooking and happy converting!

Cooking Temperature Chart

The cooking temperature chart is like your go-to recipe for getting the heat just right in your kitchen adventures. Let's explore this chart in simple terms:

1. Low Heat:

- Temperature Range: 250°F to 350°F (120°C to 175°C)

- Best For: Slow-cooking, gentle simmering, and delicate foods that need time to develop flavors.

2. Medium Heat:

- Temperature Range: 350°F to 400°F (175°C to 200°C)
- Best For: Sautéing, stir-frying, roasting vegetables, and most baking.

3. High Heat:

- Temperature Range: 400°F and above (200°C and above)
- Best For: Quick cooking, achieving crispy textures, searing meats, and creating golden-brown crusts.

Tips for Using the Cooking Temperature Chart:

- Know Your Equipment: Become familiar with your stovetop and oven to gauge the heat accurately.
- Adjust as Needed: Be ready to adjust the heat level during cooking to avoid overcooking or burning.

- **Use Timers:** Set timers to keep track of cooking times, ensuring your dishes are perfectly cooked.
- **Use Thermometers:** Use food thermometers to check internal temperatures, especially for meats and baked goods.

The cooking temperature chart is your trusty companion for mastering the art of heat in your kitchen. Embrace this handy guide, and you'll confidently navigate the temperature ranges, creating delicious dishes that will leave everyone asking for seconds.

Made in United States
Troutdale, OR
10/07/2023